Outstanding
Stands

Edition 2006

Author: Arian Mostaedi
Editorial Coordinator: Jacobo Krauel
Graphic designer & production: Dimitris Kottas
Text: contributed by the architects, edited by William George

© Carles Broto i Comerma
Jonqueres, 10, 1-5
08003 Barcelona, Spain
Tel.: +34 93 301 21 99
 Fax: +34-93-301 00 21
E-mail: info@linksbooks.net
www. linksbooks.net

Outstanding
Stands

LINKS

index

introduction

Any high-ranking company in today's business world owes its success just as much to its image as to the quality of its product. This, coupled with the considerable importance of trade shows in attracting clients, has led many companies to seek the advice of some of the leading names in contemporary architecture and design when planning their trade show stands. Hence, the birth of an entirely new discipline, combining marketing strategies and architectural creativity.

A stand must be, on the one hand, sufficiently innovative and eye-catching to attract visitors and, on the other, in perfect consonance with the product on display. Both factors are equally important; one without the other would result in an ineffective stand design.

The nearly 30 stands in this collection have been selected using this dual criteria. They are examples of some of the finest work being done in architecture today, with outstanding designs displaying creative use of technology and atypical materials; and, from a marketing perspective, they succeed in conveying the company's brand image and in attracting visitors.

From one-room stalls to sprawling multi-storied stands, representing companies as diverse as footwear, automobiles and perfume, this collection covers a spectrum of design schemes: simple and classy, technologically savvy and spectacular, young and brash, sophisticated and sublime. With work from such masters we hope to provide the reader with a thorough and reliable source of inspiration.

D'Art Design Gruppe

ACES

EuroShop 2005, Düsseldorf, Germany

Over 1500 exhibitors were present from the 19th to the 23rd of February 2005 at the Euroshop 2005, the greatest worldwide investment management tradeshow occupying about 200,000 sq.m. Within the Euro exhibition area was the international competitive show of Stand and Display Design.

An idea is only as good as its realization. That is why ACES offer optimal consulting and cost-efficient performance at every stage of a project's realization. ACES defines itself as a project management team for the realization of discriminating designs for tradeshow, shop or showroom displays.

The company's profile is clearly outlined by the planning and consulting efficiency of its executives. The worldwide presence of their displays adds to the interest of the ACES portfolio.

The task is the self presentation of ACES at the Euroshop 2005 tradeshow in Düsseldorf, to illustrate their competence as creators and installers of corporate communication stands.

The target is to use their presence at the show to communicate the company's restructured and widened strategic network. To do so, the central concerns of the enterprise will be presented and explained to the visitors and clients.

Evolution – this is the simple and concise main theme of the ACES display booth at Euroshop. The stand's designers contemplated the basic but significant question: How to describe the development and evolution of the company? The answer is captured by the concept's slogan: "Dynamics produce Change". A mobile veil moves over the stand and creates, in all the true sense of the words, temporary spaces for the main concerns of the enterprise, clearly presented at first as five stations in the form of leather cubes. These contain light boxes that offer more precise information to the visitor as he or she approaches and inspects the examples of projects and references that graphically demonstrate a clear professional pattern. The white veil moves around the cubes creating a space and volume in constant change and movement. It may even occur that the visitor and the person he is talking to, who up until then had been in an open space, find themselves inside a room. The length of the stand is only perceived in its imposing full length when the veil completely disappears. Everything must flow or »Pantha Rei«, as Heraclitus so aptly put it, and is in a constant state of development: like the company itself.

Photographs: contributed by D'Art Design Gruppe

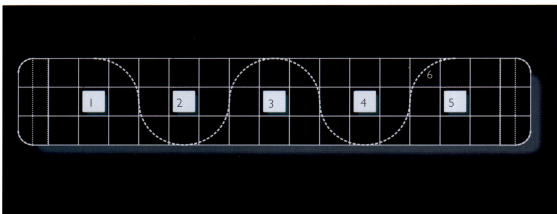

1. Stands
2. Expotools
3. Stores
4. Displays
5. Products
6. Running screen

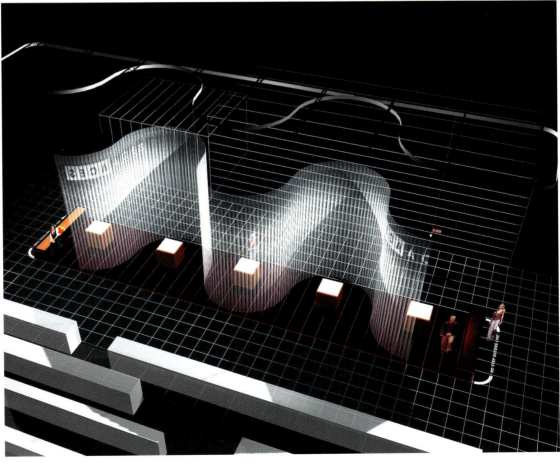

architecture:
Kauffmann Theilig & Partner
communication:
Atelier Markgraph

Daimler Chrysler AG

International Automobile Salon 2003, Geneva, Switzerland

The DC-Forum is situated in the immediate vicinity of the stand of the Mercedes, Maybach and Smart group. The Chrysler and Jeep stands do not border directly with the DC-Forum.

The DC-Forum should be clearly distinguishable from the brand stands, and any likelihood that the DC-Forum be confused with a brand stand should be avoided.

The stand consists in a rectangular cuboid volume, the dimensions of which are 15.00 x 11.00 meters and 1.50 meters high. An amoeba-like form has been cut out of the interior of the cuboid, creating a sinuous interior space that is accessible from three sides. Boldly perceivable contrasts exist between the interior and the exterior appearance of the space.

The exterior: its sharp-edged profile is clear and precise; it has a quiet and easy appearance that is directly identified with the corporate image of the group, with no further comments.

The interior: The interior is soft and atmospheric, informative and emotional, luminous and friendly, and transmits an atmosphere of warmth.

The contrast that is generated between the interior and the exterior generates a suspense that invites the spectator to look again.

Materials:

The exterior walls: The exterior walls are surfaced with aluminum foam sheeting, interrupted periodically by vertical neon joints. Top and base: aluminum foam sheeting. Floor: rolls of walkable foam (gel) covered with artificial leather. Interior walls: The interior walls consist of a screen of translucent Plexiglas in front of the LED-Panels, to backlight the whole inner perimeter with mobile and constantly changing floods of color and light. Corporate Passepartouts: The passepartouts form the frame (Corporate Group) and interfere minimally with the individual images of the brands. A ceiling structure consisting of vertically hung neon tubes located at rig level signalizes the superordinate corporate group connection. Beginning at the DC-Forum, the structure spreads over the stands of the different brands. The ceiling marker generates an individual, powerful, but, as regards the brands' intentions, not overly-dominant identifying label. The Welcome-Stelae: The welcome stelae are mounted, in the proven and known way, at the side of each brand stand's main access. The DC-Café: In this space as well, the techniques and strategies already known, tried and used in Paris and Detroit are implemented again.

Photographs: Andreas Keller, Altdorf

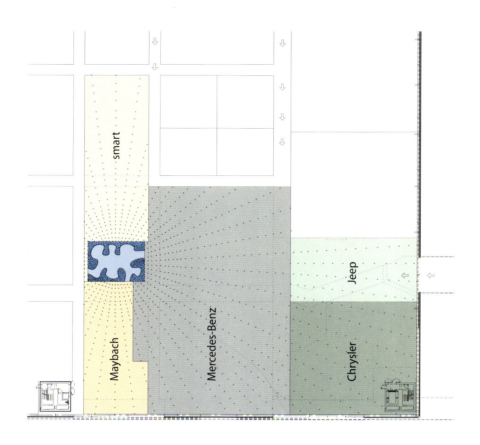

smart

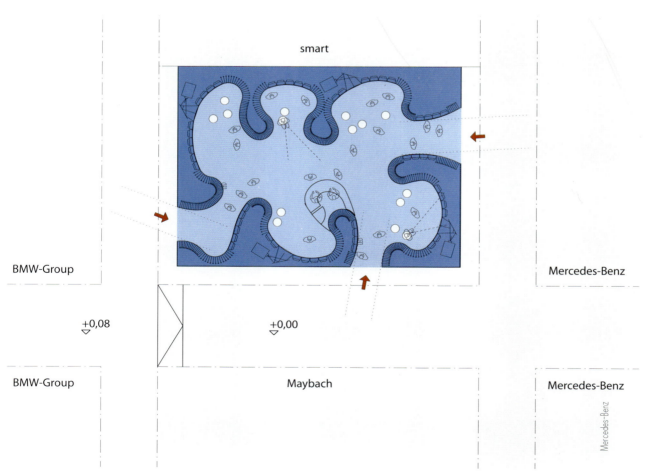

BMW-Group

Mercedes-Benz

+0,08

+0,00

BMW-Group

Maybach

Mercedes-Benz

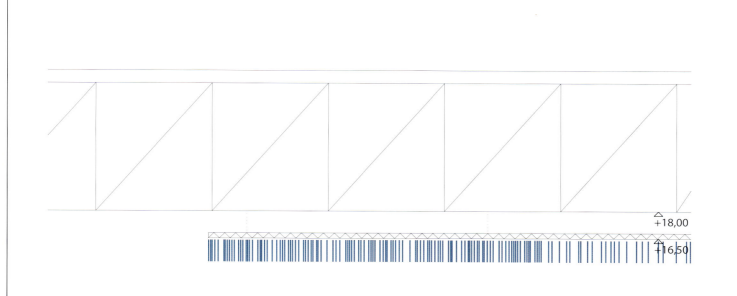

+18,00

+16,50

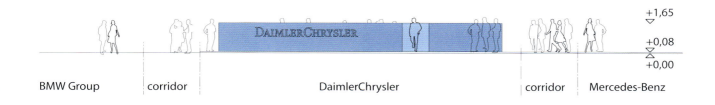

DAIMLERCHRYSLER

+1,65

+0,08
+0,00

BMW Group   corridor   DaimlerChrysler   corridor   Mercedes-Benz

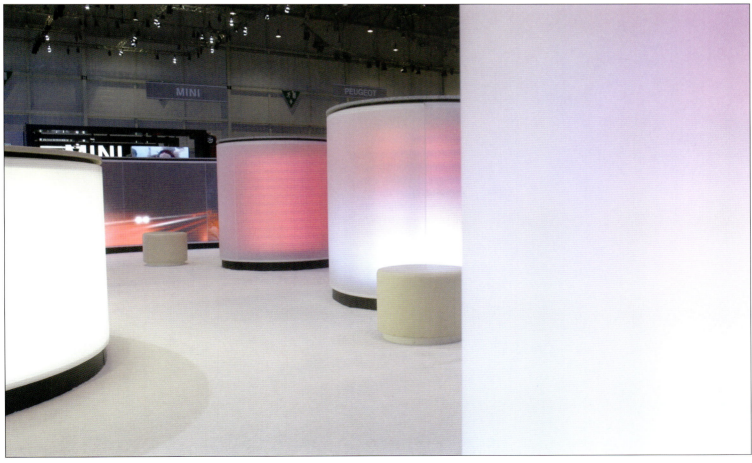

Atelier Brückner

Kodak

Photokina 2004, Cologne, Germany

Kodak anytime. anywhere, with this claim the company presented itself at Photokina 2004 as a modern service provider and competent partner for all analogue and digital photographic applications. In spite of the varied utilisations by 700 Kodak employees during the fair, the exhibition hall at Kölnmesse was consciously left a big open space, where the visitors could overlook the different exhibition and conference areas at almost any time.

Through a gallery showing networked digital products the visitors entered the exhibition hall. This open communication space was structured by a system of single "digits" - textile backlit wall units - in different sizes and colours which divided the product, conference, and presentation areas.

Three different height dimensions allowed forming differentiated areas and spaces. The "homezone" along the main ways was built out of single shear walls variantly standing and hanging which indicated private spaces. While there were presented applications for the use in public spaces and for professional purposes in the open hall, in the "homezone" Kodak products for the private use were shown.

In the centre of the hall on a surface of 25 x 6 m the visitors were received by a walkable image installation.

Two opposed overlarge three dimensional images composed out of 900 prints in all common print formats described the transition from analogue to digital photography in a pictorial way. The classical prints became pixels of a new image. This walkable "imagespace" was the most used background for snapshots at Photokina.

Photographs: contributed by Atelier Brückner

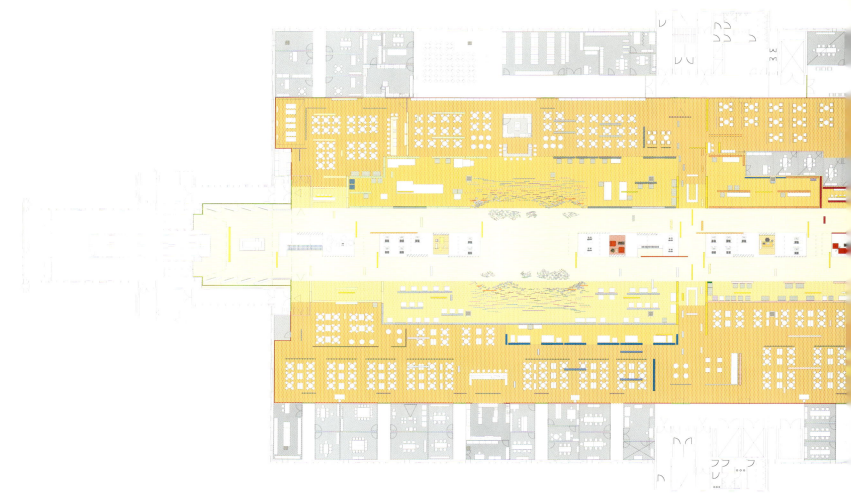

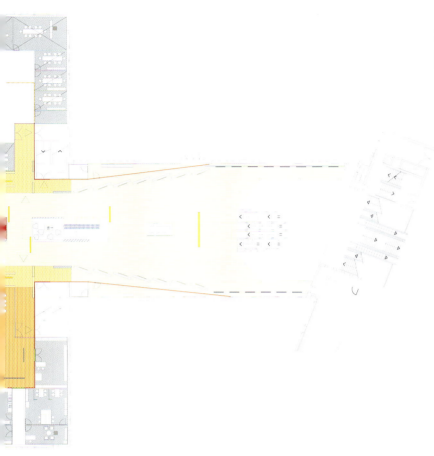

Arno Design

Kickers

various locations

The conception for the convention stand was formally coordinated with the advertising campaign and additionally developed architecturally.

"The Atmosphere of the Shooting Room" was adapted to the convention stand. An apparent transparency - a view into the lounge area - provides the opportunity to experience the "white room" in a three-dimensional fashion.

The dramaturgy of the lighting, the shadowing effect and the accent-setting red furniture in the lounge support the fundamental ideas.

This minimalist approach continues in the design of the closed areas. An apparently material-less shoe presentation (transparent Plexiglas bent into various formats) focuses the attention exclusively onto the product with no distractions. The only view inside from outside is made possible via the glass pane; a red glass pearl curtain may be able to be deployed here. Opposite the seating corner, there is a lighting box with current motifs (exchangeable); alternatively, there would be enough space here to present the Shop Window Concepts. In the external façade, integrated spotlights that can be focused provide optimum lighting and liberate us from dependence upon hanging possibilities within the convention halls.

The convention stand is constructed in a modular fashion and adaptation to various stand surfaces is no problem.

Photographs: Frank Kotzerke

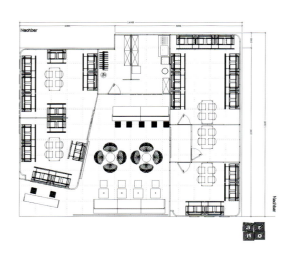

 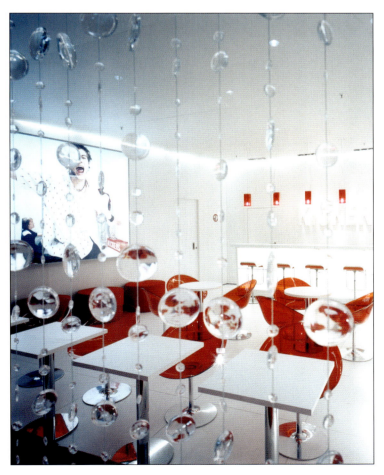

Matali Crasset

Vegetable 2005, Restaurant éphèmère

Paris, France

The Vegetable, an ephemeral place, is the restaurant that resulted from the meeting of two visions of nature and of biodiversity.

On the one hand, Alain Passard, A chef enamored of nature, who presents a floral extravaganza of tastes and aromas from his own garden, which is an expression of his philosophy of environmental respect and sustainable development (see Alain Passards's vegetable garden on the 4th floor). On the other hand, Matali Crasset, a designer who, ever since 1998, has used his work to reflect upon the meaning and the gold mine of ideas of the vegetable world. Early fruits of Matali's research were shown in full at the Institut Français in Prague, in 2003, in the context of the "Biodiversity" exhibition.

Out of this rich and unusual meeting was born a place which, like everything vegetable, is unique and ephemeral.

Photographs: Patrick Gries

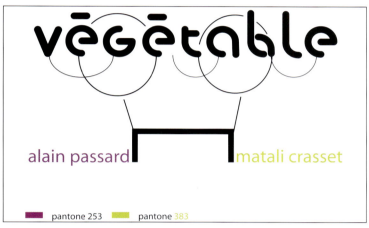

vēgētable

alain passard   matali crasset

pantone 253   pantone 383

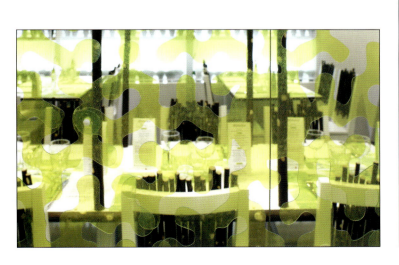

D'Art Design Gruppe

Kludi GmbH & Co. KG

ISH 2005, Frankfurt, Germany

Kludi GmbH & Co. KG is a leading international maker of quality fixtures for the bathroom and the kitchen. The brand displays a combination of attractive design and innovative technology, assembled with a modern and environment friendly production system. With a background of traditional craftsmanship, nowadays it represents creative design and state of the art casting techniques. Kludi is a many sided brand. Classical, glamorous or simply provocative, each facet has its own justification and truth. But how many variations can be presented individually yet as part of a unit?

The source of the stand's concept is to overcome the divergence between unity and plurality, thereby using an inner and outer space division: thus the plurality of the individual product worlds inside present excitement, while the outer shell establishes the unity of the brand's strength.

An outer pavilion serves as the brand's signature: porous, permeable, its openings allow views of the interior. The pavilion is a symbol of the brand's space and represents the company's pervasive concept. »Be strong where it matters« is the claim the enterprise makes and communicates visibly.

The visitors flow smoothly from one product zone to another, glittering here, colorful there, despite which the overall identity remains intact. Water fountains surround the magical world of Swarowski bathroom appliances with an air of extravagance and wealth. The Far East awaits the visitor to the Kido area, Kludi's simplified and reductionist bathroom range. Even the professional visitor can feel the quiet and relaxation here, and absorb new strength. Different facets of Kludi's idea of glamour and fascination await the visitor around every corner of the stand.

Presentation of Kludi GmbH & Co. KG at the ISH 2005 trade show in Frankfurt. Communication of their competence as makers of high quality plumbing fixtures. The show should demonstrate their role as plumbing fixture makers in the international market. The concept of Kludi's new stand places the emotional value of the brand's products in the foreground, generating an unmistakable image which carries the value of the enterprise. The challenge consisted in the variety of Kludi products, which needed to be displayed with sensitivity while reinforcing the overall identity of the brand.

Photographs: contributed by D'Art Design Gruppe

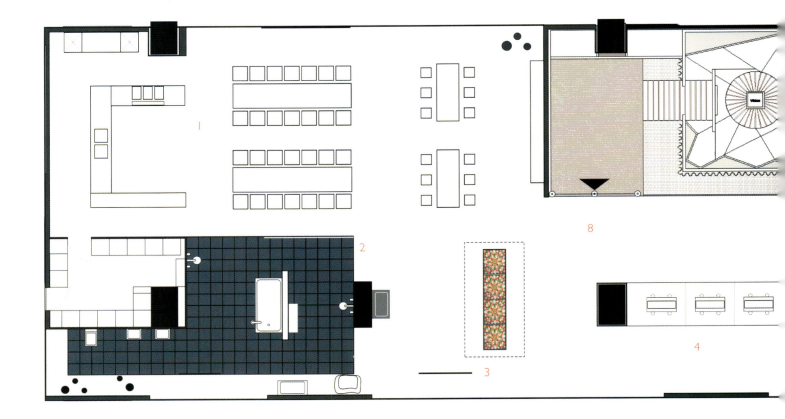

Plan

1. Catering
2. Joop!
3. Kitchen
4. Flexx-box
5. Info
6. Kidó
7. Entrance
8. Exit

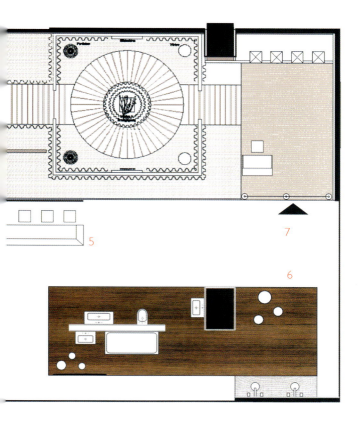

5

7

6

The Design Laboratory

The All Zones Routemaster

100% Design 2004, London, UK

Chosen to showcase London Transport's 'All Zones' interiors collection, the Routemaster bus was redesigned by the Design Laboratory at Central Saint Martins College of Art and Design.

Debuted at 100% Design, 2004, the Routemaster challenged the traditional static display stand and has since travelled across Europe introducing the All Zones collection to a variety of trade shows.

The Design Laboratory, a creative consultancy based at CSM, created six different environments on board the double decker bus to give context to Zones 1-6 of the interiors range by incorporating London Transport's classic design elements into a contemporary setting.

Based in the new Innovation Centre at Central Saint Martins, The Design Lab functions as an autonomous design studio and employs an overall team of 25 international Project Designers, drawn from a wide range of creative disciplines such as Fashion, Graphics, Media, Product, Industrial, Animation, Architecture, Spatial and Artefact. The consultancy offers clients and partners the opportunity to tap into a vibrant source of creativity that can be manifested in a variety of solutions from creative strategy, research and 'futurescaping' to communication campaigns, as well as, the design of interior environments, products, furniture, fashion and even food.

Photographs: contributed by The Design Laboratory

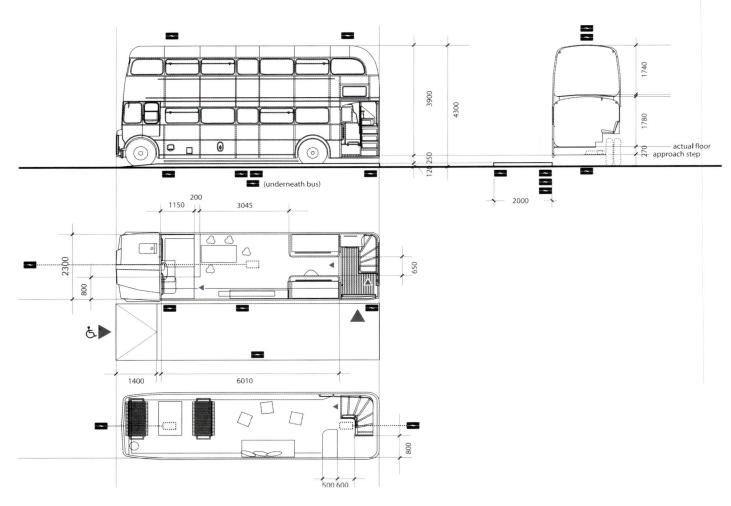

44

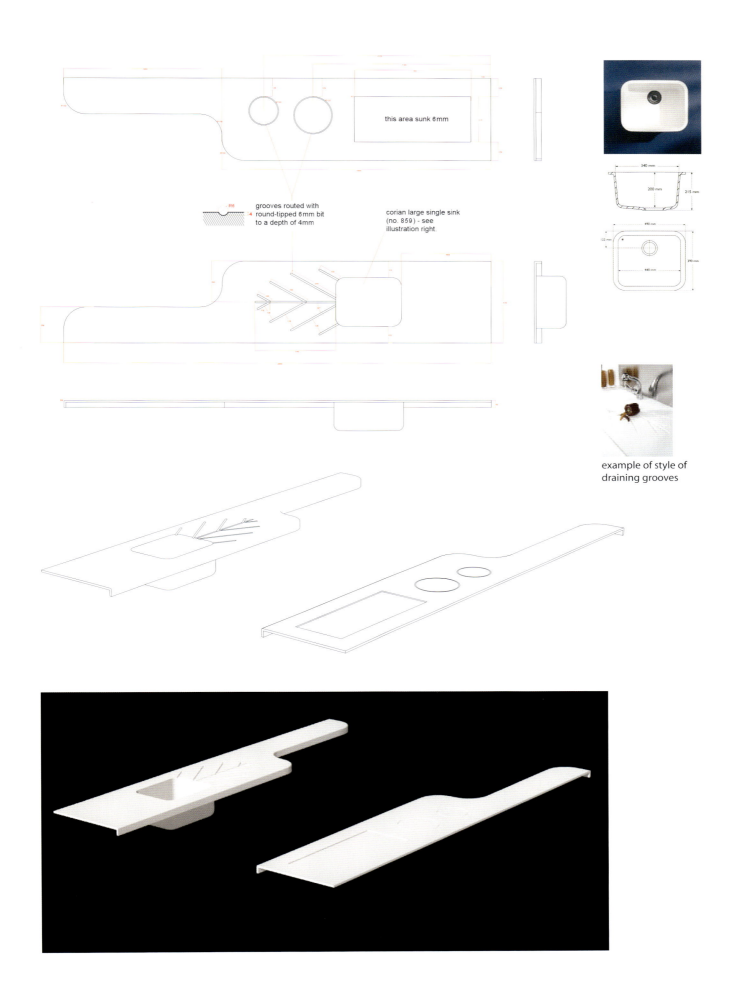

this area sunk 6mm

grooves routed with round-tipped 6mm bit to a depth of 4mm

corian large single sink (no. 859) - see illustration right.

example of style of draining grooves

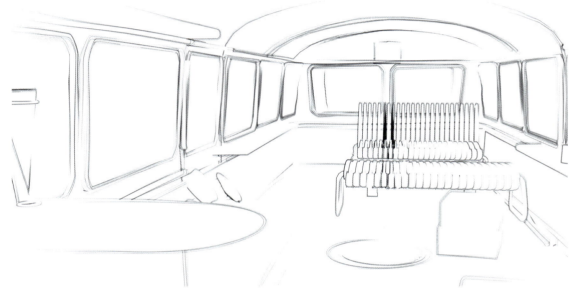

María Llerena / Cristina López-Lago

"Only with Nature"
3rd European Biennial of Landscape

Victoria convent, El Puerto de Santa María, Cádiz, Spain

The suggestive title, "Only with Nature", of the 3rd European Biennial of Landscape is a clear indication of the will to transmit the idea that landscape is the modern, sophisticated prism for reinventing our relationship with nature. The display setup in its stopover in Andalusia is an attempt to contribute to the minimizing of limits between the exterior and interior worlds of architecture, at a time when society in general and architecture specifically are exploring new relationships with nature. In order to convey this idea, images of the outside world have been projected onto the ancient walls of the building.

The program involved the creation of a renewed inner world, turning the aisle of the church into a new artificial landscape made up of a succession of wooden pleats, the logic behind the layout being read alternately as sequential (creating an itinerary, a route) or isolated (giving rise to a "field" from which the displays emerge). Making use of the red carpet coating the aisle, the pleats become sinuous tongues that threatened to rebel and reveal a new relationship with the ancient Gothic-era walls.

These forms comprise the backdrop to the projections designed by the planning committee; and the pleats are meant to accommodate visitors, while destabilizing any static view of architecture.

Photographs: Fernando Alda

S.

suports / soportes / supports

14
finalistes / finalistas / nominations

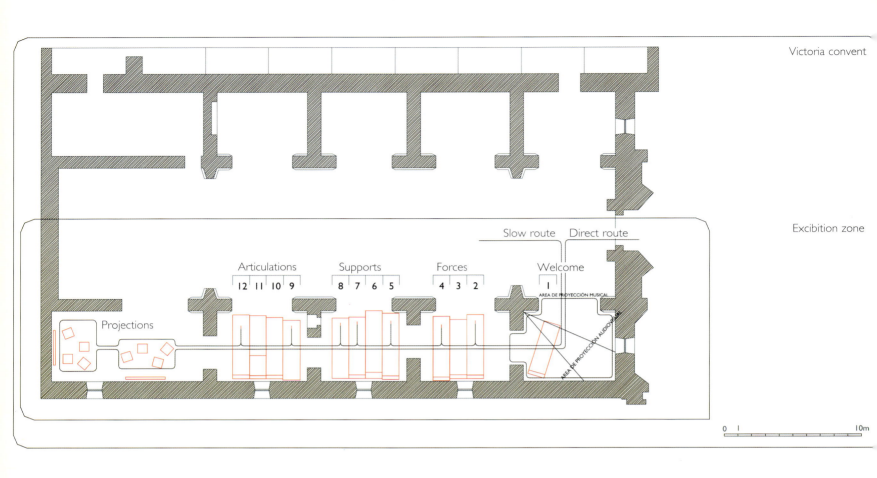

Victoria convent

Excibition zone

Slow route   Direct route

Articulations   Supports   Forces   Welcome
12 11 10 9   8 7 6 5   4 3 2   1
AREA DE PROYECCIÓN MUSICAL

Projections

AREA DE PROYECCIÓN AUDIOVISUAL

0 1   10m

Aisle 2

Plan

n.4
n.3
n.2

Section

2

pieza n.2_nave 2_desarrollo: 7,2m.

3

pieza n.3_nave 2_desarrollo: 6,2m.

4

pieza n.4_nave 2_desarrollo: 6,9m.

Elevation

2 3 4

0 1   6m

Sections

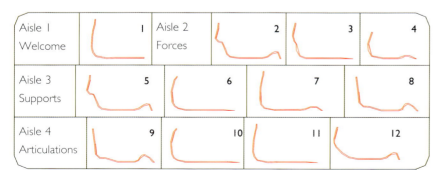

Aisle 1 Welcome	1	Aisle 2 Forces	2	3	4
Aisle 3 Supports	5	6	7	8
Aisle 4 Articulations	9	10	11	12

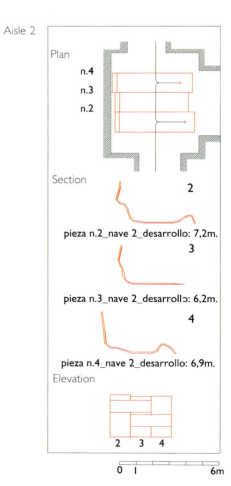

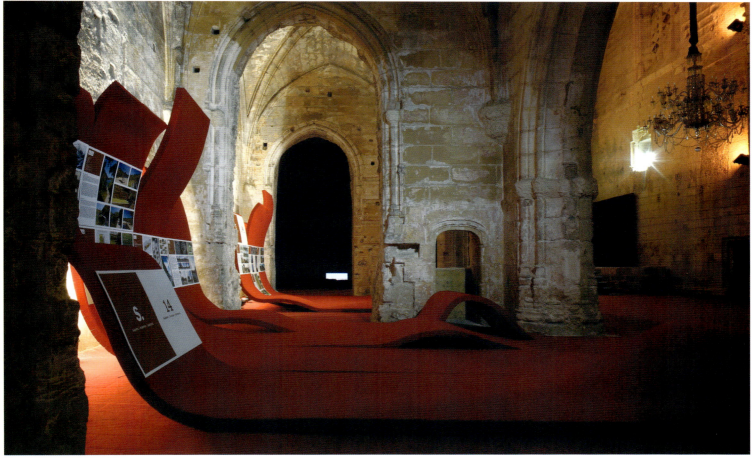

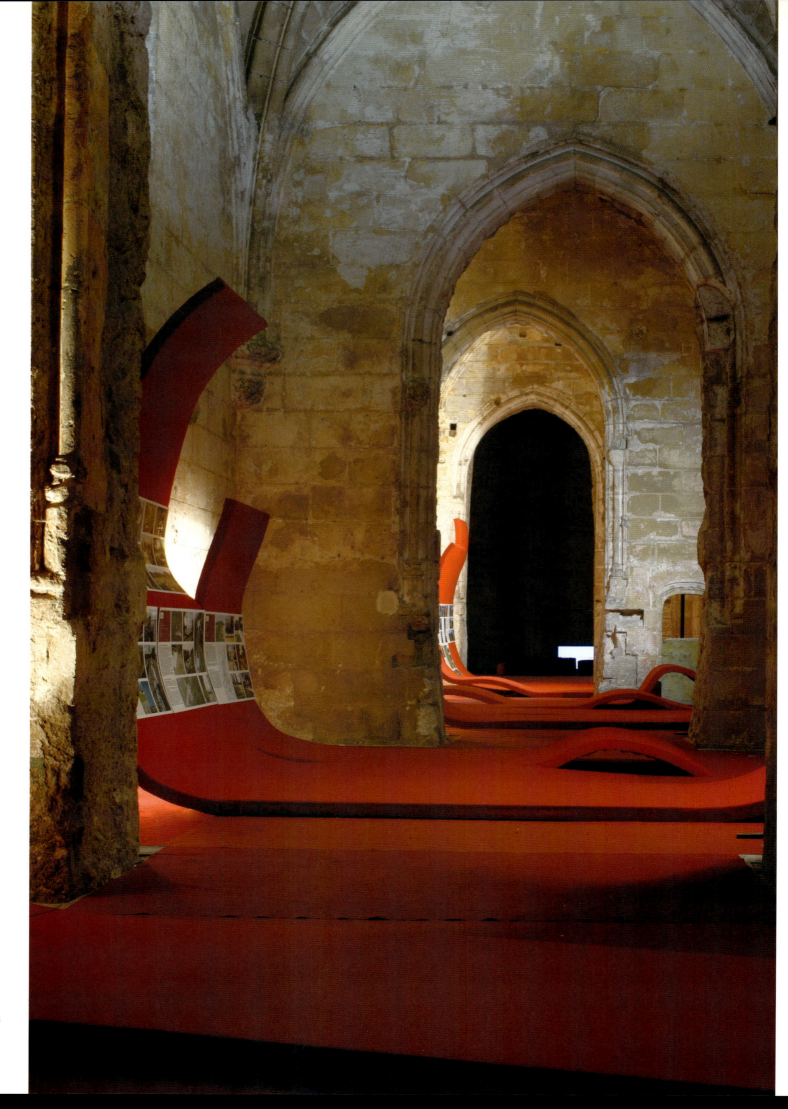

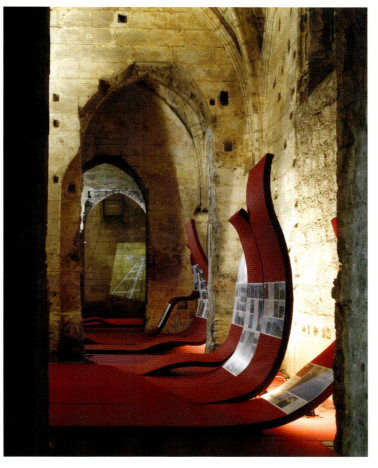

Formpol AG

Bodenschatz

Swissbau 2005, Basel, Switzerland

Taking care of the body, feeling good and relaxing have become essential parts of our everyday lives and of our quality of living. Today, the bathroom is as much the place for our personal care and hygiene as the sanctuary of our relaxation and wellbeing.

The old bathroom we always knew has undergone a contemporary transformation, to give its users the heightened emotional value that they require, at the same level as the living room or the bedroom. This evolution demands a new way of thinking about the design and utilization of these spaces.

In this context, the Swiss firm Bodenshatz has developed their RIVA range of bathroom fixtures and accessories, with which it is entering the field of bathroom accessories, to which it intends to bring the particular philosophy of design it has promoted in other areas: functionality, understood in the widest sense of the word. This range of products was presented for the first time at the Bodenschatz stand at the Swissbau 05 tradeshow.

The stand presented four stylized bathrooms of different sizes, colors and fixtures. To do so their display area was divided into four autonomous spaces, four independent light-flooded cubes, identified by their color which lends each of them its particular emotional and atmospheric punch. This analytical way of distributing the stand illustrates the spirit of the enterprise, whose products embody a synthesis of the pragmatically technological and the emotional. This isn't the first collaboration between Bodenschatz and the designers Hanspeter Wirth and Suzanne Marti, of Formpol; they have previously conducted research into the field of verifiable methods of measuring the quality of a design. The stand intends to share this clarity with the visitors, and does so by means of a visible reduction of theatrical paraphernalia: in such a minimalistic context the links between function and emotion can be clearly perceived and appreciated.

Both the fixtures and the floors and walls of the illuminated cubes have been designed in a symbolic and abstract manner. This strategy permits the taps and accessories to take center stage, manifesting in various ways the credo of the enterprise: aesthetics and ergonomics. That is: emotion and science.

Photographs: contributed by Formpol AG

Kurz und Partner Architekten

DaimlerChrysler AG

International Automobil-Salon 2005, Geneva, Switzerland

A wide Mercedes-Benz sculpture extends itself over the provided hall rear wall. The brand appearance of Maybach is integrated in the sculptures right side. A prominent cut in the center of the sculpture presents the world premier of the B-Class.

The main Mercedes-Benz sign with its star and its word mark are positioned above the area of the sportstourer presentation. Two more stars can be found to the left and right side. The blue pylon is placed in the open area in the front. The silver center part of the building is illuminated and has a built –in LED screen. An elevated platform presenting the B-Class and the R-Vision as well as two turntables, faces on the side the Mercedes-Benz communication foyer and on the other side the SLR lounge.

The upper part of the cladding is encased with a passepartout made of black rhombs.

On the first floor of the Mercedes-Benz sculpture is the DaimlerChrysler Café, another location of the new M-Class resembles the design of the B-Class platform. Next to it the service suppliers can be found like the shop counter and the brochure counter. The voluminous vehicles (E-Class an C-Class) as well as the Viano are placed in this area of the stand.

Black communication elements with built-in benches divide the stand into areas where the different vehicle groups are positioned.

The Maybach main stand element is a dynamically altered cube built of ivory-colored flowstone.

The entrance is clearly defined by an eye-catching glass wall with orange gaps. The word mark of Maybach in neon lights is positioned on the front façade. Two more chromed word marks with badges are placed on either side of the cube.

Photographs: Andreas Keller Fotografie

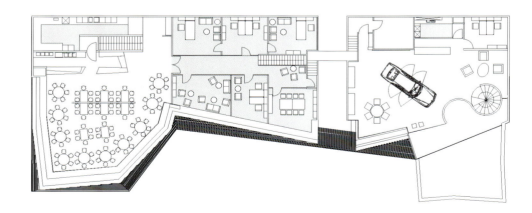

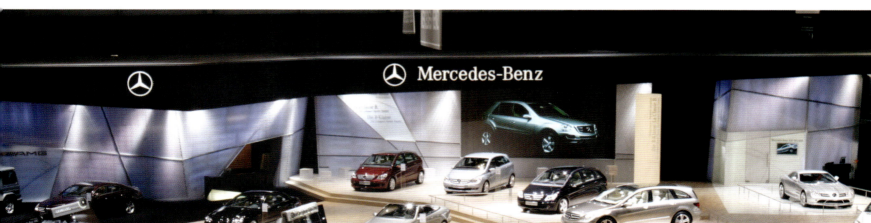

Simone Micheli

The first touch of Liri ®evolution

Decosit, 2004, Brussels, Belgium

Liri ®evolution, a section of experimental activity and decorative-material research of Liri Industriale, has presented its first creative performance at the exhibition "Italian Suite Hotel", curated by Architect Simone Micheli, on the occasion of the Deco Contract 2004 in Brussels, shouting "through an effervescent idea of laminate it is possible to give new breath to the project of architecture, to the project of design" !

The exhibition, that has brought the attention through the stimulation of a "charming suite" with bath of a hotel characterized by new functional content, clear white colorations, multiple transparencies and reflections, and macro decorations of brilliant colors, has shown Liri ®evolution in its first performance in the vast world of the possible.

Architect Micheli, with his unmistakable and biting touch, curated this three dimensional performance linked to the dematerialization of the limits between the room and the bath in a hotel, celebrating materials, valorizing their merits and their particularities, with the basic objective of suggesting renewed ideas related to content and an infinite number of possible interpretations to the observer.

All prototypes, materials and design, together with the essential forms, colors, lights, sounds, and smells, represented the indispensable ingredients for the creation of a three dimensional environment of a notable visual impact.

Liri ®evolution participated in this performance of interior design with fascinating and exhilarating "signs of laminate", created by Simone Micheli, applied to the surfaces of the walls and to a large armoire with a double desk. The digital press Personal Image on laminate "Priv-Standard HPL", used for the exhibition, represented the stylization of a world of macro-flowers of bright colors, generating an enthusiastic graphic-spatial alteration an offering new ideas for a sleeping world to make.

Participating in the realization of the event in co-sponsor with Liri Industriale were: Adrenalina, Baumann dekor, Kasthall, Conceira Chiorino, Consorzio Mobili, Mascioni, Italamp, MP2, Hoesch, Fratelli Fantini, Crassveig and Oikos Fragrances.

Photographs: contributed by Simone Micheli

Schmidhuber + Partner

Grohe

ISH 2005, Frankfurt, Germany

The idea: The seminal idea of the new project for the client's tradeshow stand at ISH 2005 is based on the theme of "flowing water" to represent the main subject in which Grohe Water Technology is competent.

The realization: The subject of flowing permeates all the areas of the display and projects this image to the tradeshow:

• Translated into the two-dimensional graphic expression of the brands leit-motiv, it takes the ultimate form of moving water: the wave.

• The three-dimensional translation of the flowing theme is spatial: "Fluid"

• The ordering principle of the display modules is dynamic: the "Streamlines".

The unification: The "Fluid" itself is perceived as a spatial element that identifies the show stand, and the meaning of which unmistakably linked to Grohe and which sets it apart from the rest of the commercial environment. The "Fluid" is no flat translation of Grohe's logo, it is an interpretation of the main subject of Grohe Water Technology's field of expertise: flowing water.

The branding: The "Fluid" is a carrier for the Grohe-Logo, strengthening and underlining its profile at the tradeshow.

The call: The "Fluid", with its unmistakable flowing form and its activation with light is the sign that is seen from a distance in the exhibition space, and awakens the visitor's curiosity and interest from afar.

The atmosphere: Within the immediate experience of the Grohe display stand, the "Fluid" becomes a space dividing and organizing solution. The color climate in blues and greens and varying intensity of the light create a unique atmosphere, which contributes to communicate the main theme of "flowing water".

The sinuously curved three-dimensional "Streamlines", of different heights and lengths, display both sides of the products, most of them actively pouring water. The linear distribution of the "streamlines" underlines the theme of flowing.

The installation: The two and three dimensional elements of the presentation, the streamlines and the fluid, have such an indelible effect that they can even influence the reading of other elements at the show. The stand is a complete achievement regarding its projection of a ubiquitous and highly recognizable image of every aspect of the brand's products, a new corporate architecture.

Photographs: Eberhard Franke, München

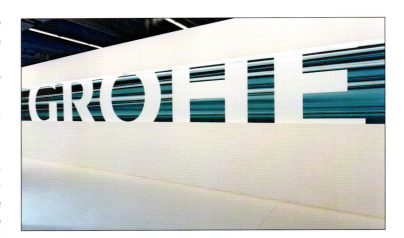

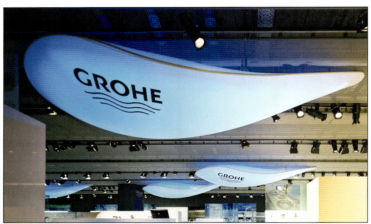 

Bottega + Ehrhardt Architekten

Burgbad AG

ISH 2005 Frankfurt, Germany

Clarity and reduction are the main characteristics of the architecture of the new exhibition stand for Burgbad AG, presented the first time on the ISH 2005 in Frankfurt. The outer skin is open and closed at the same time, allows a variety of different views into the stand and strenghten the curiosity of the visitor discovering the new world of Burgbad.

A modular principle out of differently placed and stapled wooden volumes builds the outer skin. This refers to the companys history, originally producing boxes of wooden building blocks for children. The inner skin is made out of natural bamboo with a height of 9 meters, forming an atrium in the center of the stand and creating a filter towards the exhibition spaces of the three different brands Burg, Kama and Schock. All of them unified in the atrium as central space of communication.

Photographs: KD Busch Fotostudio

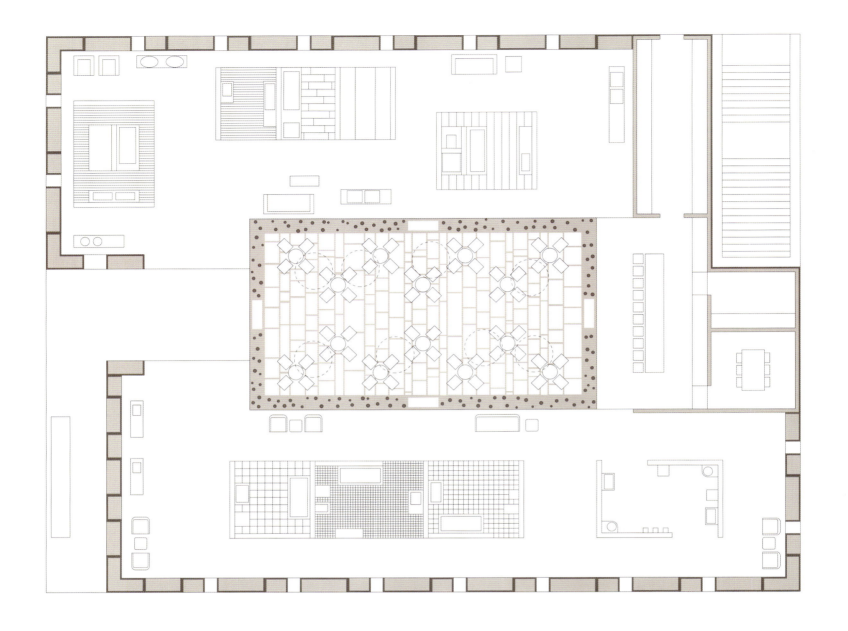

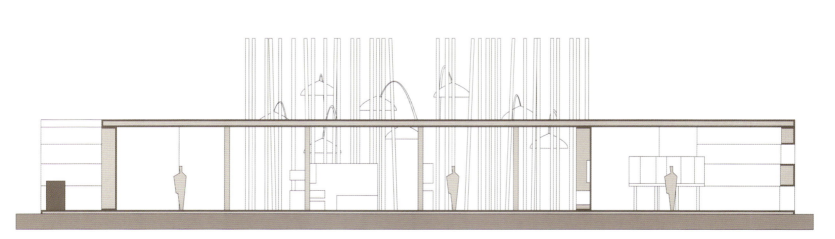

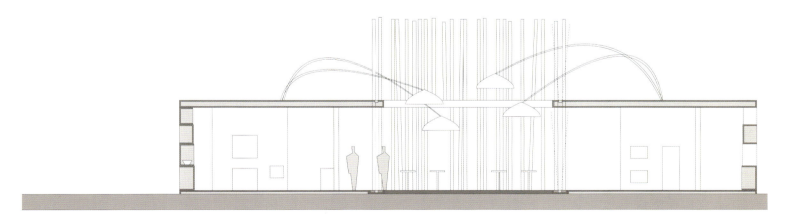

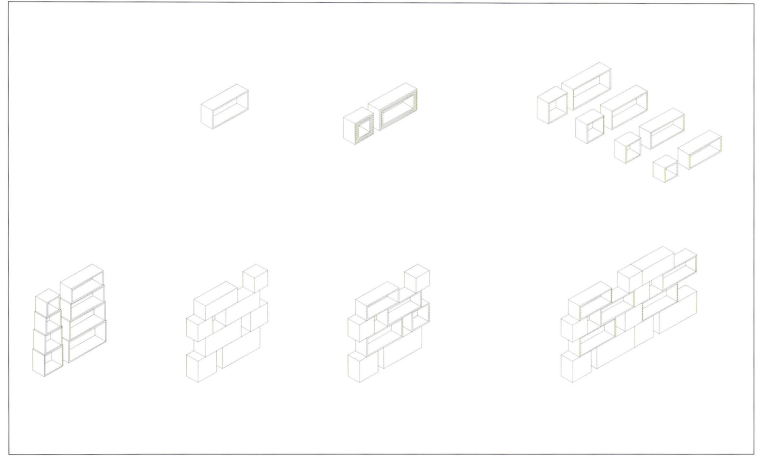

Arno Design

Auto Art Graz

Graz, Austria

Graz enjoys a worldwide reputation as a top location for automotive engineering. 35 top examples of "auto art" in the Stadthalle demonstrated that car design may also be a form of art. The "auto art" exhibition united car enthusiasts and people interested in culture. The history of car design has seen many models that were also interesting from an artistic point of view. For the first time an exhibition focused on the highlights of creative car design, presenting an impressive number of showcars - prototypes featuring utopian components. They were intended as product studies, which are not always produced for the market afterwards.

Barcelona-based international car designer Erwin Himmel, the initiator and curator of this exhibition, calls showcars "the stars of automotive art and the precursors of future automobile generations". His exhibition - sponsored by the Province of Styria (Department of Economy, Finance and Telecommunication) - welcomed visitors to his world, presenting 35 show cars of all important manufacturers on an area of over 7,000 square metres an overview of different cultural and temporal styles in automotive history. The supporting programme included topic-related activities as well as many surprises.

Photographs: Frank Kotzerke

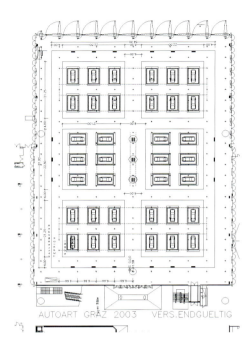

AUTOART GRAZ 2003   VERS.ENDGUELTIG

BWM Architekten und Partner

XAL

Light Fair 2003, New York, USA
Light + Building 2004, Frankfurt, Germany

Xenon Architectural Lighting, a firm designing and producing architectural lighting fixtures and appliances, required the creation of an exhibition stand for a New York trade show, the Light Fair 2003.

The space is occupied by an entirely enclosed volume, despite which the permeable and soft outer skin offers a sensitive surface to the passing visitors. The walls glow with a warm light that awakens the spectators' curiosity and draws them into the space where the firm's products are displayed and its ideas are communicated. XAL is represented as a colorfully illuminated textile shell, soft on the outside but containing precision displays of light on the inside. Thus the shape and the material texture of the stand illustrate the two facets of the image of the enterprise, state of the art technology and ethereal sensitivity. The stand represents light made solid and tangible, light as the vehicle of experience and enjoyment, the tactile quality of illumination.

Light is transformed into a graphic projection. The graphic presence of the stand is achieved by the arrangement of lights on the inside which appear as forms that radiate the hazy material, generating a colorful pattern of subtle luminous hues that soak through the slightly convex outer textile shell, which seems to hardly resist the tendency to spill into the dark exterior.

BWM Architects and Partners were contracted by XAL to create an exhibition space to present its product ranges at the Frankfurt Light and Building Trade Show 2004. The volume was to evoke the symbolic guidelines that determine the firm's aesthetic position and identity, while capturing the ethereal qualities of the materials which they work with: energy and light. The space had to become the communication center of the enterprise for the duration of the show, as well as its visual and formal representation.

Visual communication takes the shape of a colorfully illuminated light cube demonstrating the close relationship between space, color and light. Nevertheless the rigor of the cube's 'platonic' geometry is mollified by the inflated, elastically curved volume of the walls that define the space; added to which their glowing and translucent appearance illustrate the intangible nature of light contained and controlled by the geometry of design: a soft organic sensuousness contrasts excitingly with the sharp edged quality of the dominating forms, inviting the visitors to enter the enjoyable game of hues and shapes. Colored lines of light, centrally controlled, create atmospheric moods of light on the inside as well as on the outside of the cube. On the inside, twelve white cubes float in space, forming the essential and focused setting of the product presentation.

Photographs: XAL

Caramel architekten + Friedrich Stiper

The AMI Booth - Agrolinz Melamine International

K04, October 2004, Düsseldorf, Germany

With the aim of counteracting the hectic bustle and over-stimulation one finds in the exhibition setting, a "space inside a space" was created, which by virtue of its colors and acoustic properties radiates tranquility and safety and encourages visitors to linger.

The colors of the textile surfaces are the same as those of the company logo. The triple loops also correspond to the AMI logo.

The loop ends constitute the two access zones; the association of a "red carpet" punctuates the overall gesture.

Depending on the angle, this constructed space seems open or closed. The spatial structure is a freestanding object within the consciously withdrawn, standard dividing walls consisting of white curtains that bear only the letters of the company logo.

In the interior space there is a row of stand-up tables, where visitors can consult with company representatives. Those who prefer being passively informed from a more comfortable position can relax in front of a row of screens that play AMI info films. For each screen there is a fold-out seat that can be "peeled" out of the inner shell of the spiral. The comfortable seating position encourages visitors to take off their coats and stay a while.

The lighting inside the booth contributes significantly to the spatial atmosphere. Points of light directed at the stand-up tabletops communicate with linear rails, which hold the mandatory sprinkler system as well as the indirect lighting, illuminating the table surfaces without glare.

The spatial structure consists of a two-layered, lightweight wooden construction consisting of five prefabricated parts per loop. Each section can be handled by 2-3 persons and houses the ducts for the lighting and IT systems.

The individual sections can be assembled in a short time and are reusable. They are covered with a layer of textile, felt-like material or imitation black leather.

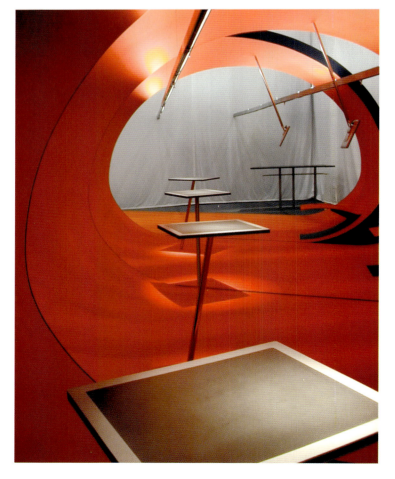

Photographs: contributed by Caramel

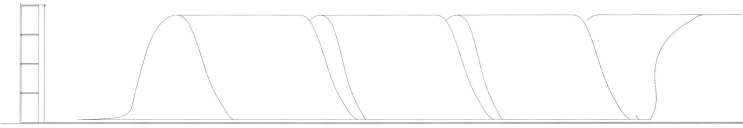

storage | consulting | presentation tables | interactive information | recreation / extra consulting | textile wall

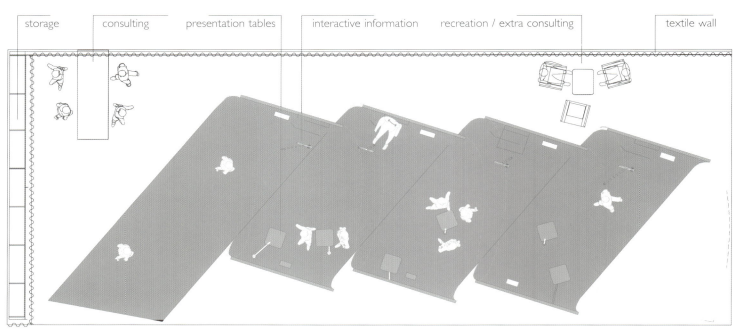

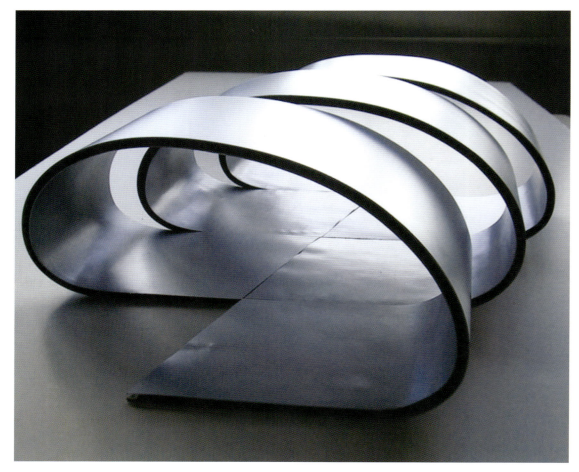

92

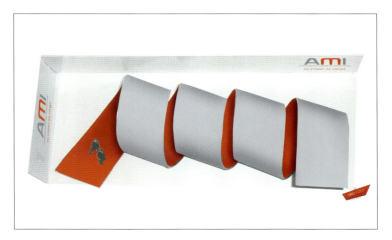
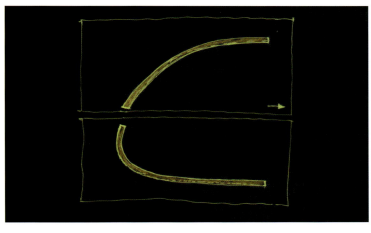
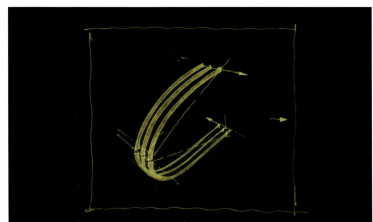
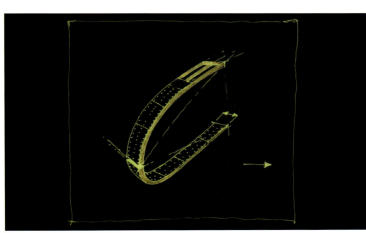
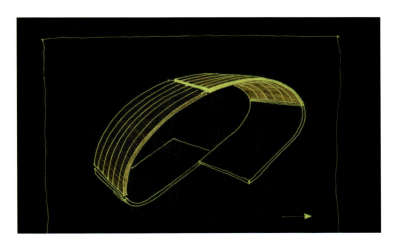
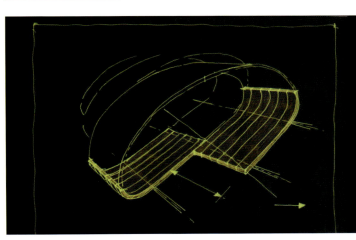
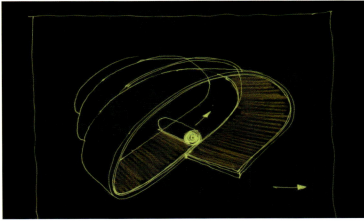

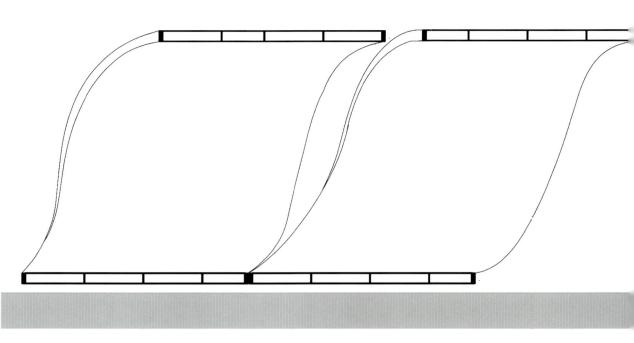

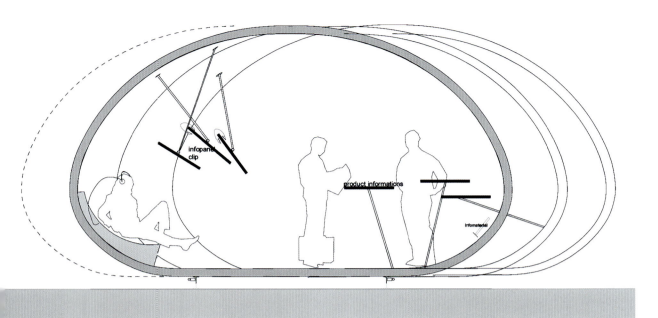

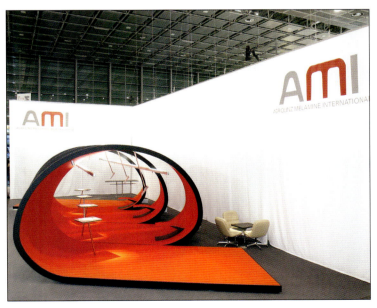

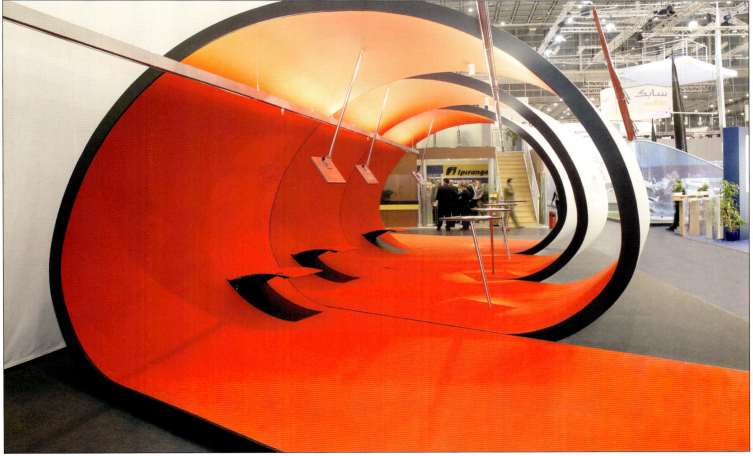

Schmidhuber + Partner

Audi

Internationaler Automobilsalon, 2005, Geneva, Swizerland

At the Automobile Show in Geneva, the Audi stand focused on the 25 year jubilee of their quattro® technology and on their new RS4 –the High Performance Version of the Audi A4 series.

The new RS4, the only element in red, is displayed on a central lane, slightly raised above the main floor. In front of it, an illustrious ancestor, the original 1980 Audi quattro®, represents the foundation stone of the brand's success. The Audi Models are displayed to the left and right of the highlight lane. The special position and presentation of the Silver Metal series shows the all-round versatility of the series and communicates its upper range value and prestige. '4 Dimensions' stands for the four quattro® themes: security, dynamics, technology and history. The new RS4 is the manifestation of all four quattro® themes in one car. Four cubical sensation islands enable visitors to experience with their own bodies what there is behind the quattro® technology.

Safety Installation: Six luxurious deckchairs allow the visitors to relax while the chairs revolve slowly, looking in through the top of the cube to see a high resolution projected animation representing various weather conditions, designed to communicate the feeling of safety offered to Audi drivers by the quattro® technology.

Heritage Installation: A 270° sensurround film installation on 20 full-size screens makes the visitor part of the quattro® history, sitting next to Walter Röhrl as he races around the rally courses, celebrating with Hans Joachim Stuck the victories on the American race courses.

Technology Installation: In four glass pedestals the visitor is challenged to physically take over the quattro®'s distribution system. Hands and feet feel the distribution of the force simulated by the vehicle's computerized drive system, experiencing how the car's technology reacts intelligently to changing road conditions.

Dynamics Installation: The visitor can physically experience the type of improvement a quattro® powered car embodies in comparison with front or back wheel drive vehicles. He is offered the opportunity of driving up the 60% gradient seen in the famous T.V. commercial. Different positions of the driver seat simulate the car's relation to different power drive concepts.

The multipurpose building also contains a generous cafeteria and lounge, separated from the other areas by a semitransparent screen. Lecture rooms are available, and the 'Audi Exclusive' lounge, presents individualized possibilities for the different models. The backdrop of the stand displays the recognizable Audi colors.

Photographs: Andreas Keller, Altdorf

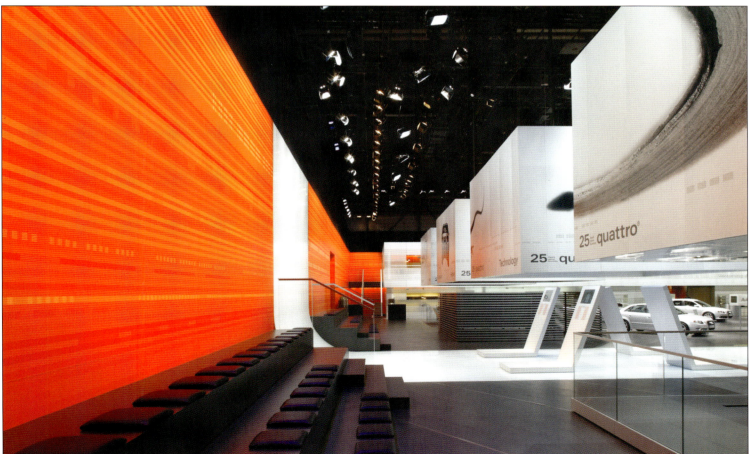

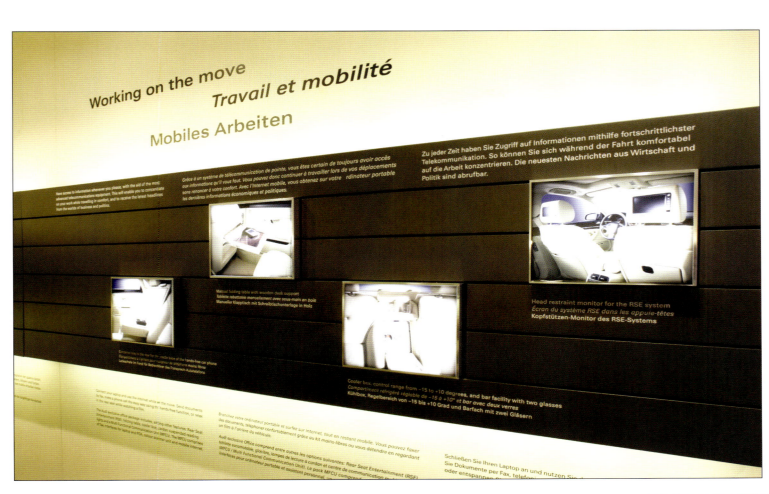

Working on the move
Travail et mobilité
Mobiles Arbeiten

Zu jeder Zeit haben Sie Zugriff auf Informationen mithilfe fortschrittlichster Telekommunikation. So können Sie sich während der Fahrt komfortabel auf die Arbeit konzentrieren. Die neuesten Nachrichten aus Wirtschaft und Politik sind abrufbar.

Manual folding table with wooden desk support
Tablette rabattable manuellement avec sous-main en bois
Manueller Klapptisch mit Schreibtischunterlage in Holz

Head restraint monitor for the RSE system
Écran du système RSE dans les appuie-têtes
Kopfstützen-Monitor des RSE-Systems

Cooler box, control range from −15 to +10 degrees, and bar facility with two glasses
Compartiment réfrigéré réglable de −15 à +10° et bar avec deux verres
Kühlbox, Regelbereich von −15 bis +10 Grad und Barfach mit zwei Gläsern

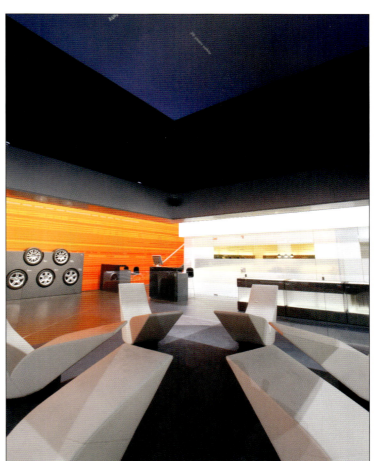

Burkhardt Leitner constructiv + Fleichman & Kirsch

Flowing Office - Spaces Communication Acoustics

ORGATEC 2004, Frankfurt, Germany

As a place of social contact and corporate cultural experience, the office is a centre of communication. The more communication is emphasized, however, whether over the phone or in person, the more acoustic disturbance arises. At the same time, the increasingly creative focus on knowledge processing requires a degree of concentration not needed in purely manual activities. The communication-oriented infrastructure of modern offices requires acoustically shielded meeting areas, while maintaining visual openness.

Burkhardt Leitner constructiv addresses these challenges by launching innovative modular architectural acoustic systems that prove their creative expertise in spatial acoustics: modern spatial concepts with innovative acoustic solutions that allow for flexible integration into existing architectural systems – from felt-covered, sound-absorbing PE acoustic panels and powder-coated compound baffle absorbers (developed in co-operation with the Fraunhofer Institute in Stuttgart), to transparent high tech material dividers, acoustic fabric panels, or micro-perforated and sound-absorbing film panels.

The mobile OfficeBox, by constructiv PILA Office, is the self-sufficient office taken to its logical conclusion – completely equipped with electrical modules for integral data and network connectivity, with desk, and shelving units. Modular acoustic panels may be hung at any height and quantity, reducing reverberation time by up to a quarter. As an acoustically shielded think tank, or a mobile work station, the OfficeBox is a glimpse of tomorrow's temporary office serving the hypermobility of job nomads as well as the need for intimate working environments. The transparent constructiv PILA Office MeetingBox uses a range of different acoustic modules to guarantee an undisturbed atmosphere in which to conduct meetings, but also an uninterrupted flow of communication between interior and exterior.

The Burkhardt Leitner constructiv installation at Orgatec 2004 presented a sample setup of various acoustically shielded communication and concentration zones, built with the constructiv PILA Office architectural system. These provided a conclusive demonstration of the system's modular and versatile adaptability to the space available and to changing office structures – thereby enabling the work space to constantly reinvent itself. The show's success has proved Burkhardt Leitner right. The stand underlined mobility and acoustics in the modern office as their theme– effectively estimating contemporary concern for a subject that aroused general interest.

The entire range of this internationally acclaimed office system was exhibited and demonstrated its versatility as flexible »flowing office« architecture – from shelving systems, cupboard doors, and lighting systems to suspended filing systems, and more. The newly developed desk with integral lamp attracted considerable interest. The worktop sits on two constructiv CLIC Office containers which offer generous storage for computer and office supplies. Add shelving systems, lowboards, and sideboards, and the entire constructiv CLIC Office effortlessly appears... An office that is also a tradeshow stand representing tself.

Photographs: Lothar Bertrams

Bonjoch Associats

Escola Elisava

Saló de l'Ensenyament 2004, Fira de Barcelona, Spain

Barcelona'a Escola de Disseny Elisava was presented as an open book in the educational trade show "Saló de l'Ensenyament". Light and space have been masterfully combined in this stand, creating a relaxed atmosphere, an isolated bubble within the chaos that ordinarily reigns at trade shows.

The different parts of the stand have been designed to make it look like a book resting on the very floor of the pavilion. A curved wall simulates the spine, where larger than life sized letters and logo reinforce the corporative presence of the design school, while at the same time providing a "title" for the book and guiding visitors wishing to obtain information about the institution. The floor and roof of the stand are the back and front covers, with the pages of the book symbolically alluded to by slightly separated strips of wood backlit by fluorescent tubes. From the outside, glowing beams of light filter through the strips of wood, framing the stand and giving it the singularity and authority befitting of the school's standards of excellence.

Access to the stand is via two openings at the sides. The interior is characterized by visual cleanliness, consolidated by the straight lines and the white that impregnates every corner of the space. This appearance is a nod to the concept of a "blank page", that challenge that sooner or later each of the students of this school will be faced with.

Two tables occupy the lengthwise central space of the stand and, along with a bench that crosses the entire area, comprise the stand's informational point. The "Panton" chairs, with their deep red tone, break the prevailing silence and send a cry into the space, representing the first sketches of the projects that will one day be etched onto paper.

Photographs: contributed by Bonjoch Associats

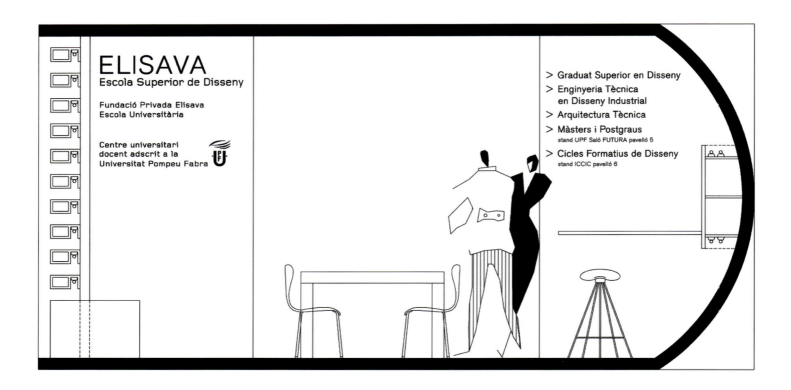

ELISAVA
Escola Superior de Disseny

Fundació Privada Elisava
Escola Universitària

Centre universitari
docent adscrit a la
Universitat Pompeu Fabra

> Graduat Superior en Disseny
> Enginyeria Tècnica
  en Disseny Industrial
> Arquitectura Tècnica
> Màsters i Postgraus
  stand UPF Saló FUTURA pavelló 5
> Cicles Formatius de Disseny
  stand ICCIC pavelló 6

Section

ippolito fleitz group

RÖWA

Internationale Möbelmesse 2004, Köln, Germany

Rössle & Wanner, a leading German bed systems manufacturer, have extended their field from slatted frames and mattresses to a new range of system beds, connecting the ergonomics and comfort of the RÖWA bed systems with high-grade design.

The firm's stand at the 2004 furniture show, Cologne, presented the new line and the introduced the RÖWA trademark to the furniture market.

The stand had to fulfill the following tasks:

- Stage-managing the stand.
- Communicating the change from bed systems to system-beds.
- Representing the RÖWA trademark's values: detailed finish, functionality, and high quality

The stand has three zones: showcase, forum, product intensification.

Zone A (Showcase) is the stand's most prominent area. Visible from a distance at the end of the aisle, its floor is raised above an illuminated step. The products' facets are displayed in three brightly lit Plexiglas cylinders. A freehanging frame shows the well thought-out and aesthetic class of the product. The third cylinder displays an exploded bed with all individual parts dismembered and suspended in space with transparent threads. The aesthetics of the 'system-bed' are easily related to the ergonomics of the 'bed-system'. The three cylinders attract visitors to the RÖWA stand, but the stand's prominence by the escalator is offset by the fact that two-thirds of it are in a niche. An S-shaped backboard enlivens the background.

After the visual opening of zone A, visitors rise another step to zone B (forum), where a bright, friendly area invites conversation. Three cubic pedestals display the framework systems. The back-lit display, well-chosen colors and visibility guarantee coherence between the three-dimensional stage set and the picture language of printed communication.

Finally, in zone C (product intensification), under two large black volumes, two beds are available for testing. The two floating volumes define the beds' positions and simultaneously illuminate them. Visitors testing the beds look up at the back-lit logo of the campaign. The bedclothes are spotlighted to form a colorful, sensuous background to the spatial choreography.

The three zones are outlined by their different levels. In zone A, the strong visual opening puts the product in center stage. The cylinders contain and radiate light, but the linoleum floor around them is dark and two-dimensional. Zone B looks spacious, bright and subtle. The impression is enhanced by a large skylight, an invitation to linger; the floor here consists of several parts, a pattern of pale gray MDF. There is an all-round view of the stand from here. Zone C takes us back to inspect the product again. Light falls in patches on the beds and the textile collection. The backlit view of the beds closes the series with a strong visual statement.

The materials reflect the products' clarity and precision as well as comfortable sophistication, contrasting transparent Plexiglas and soft vistas, enameled surfaces and textiles (lamp shades, cylinder tops), sharp-edged objects and padded backgrounds (zone A, C).

Photographs: Zooey Braun

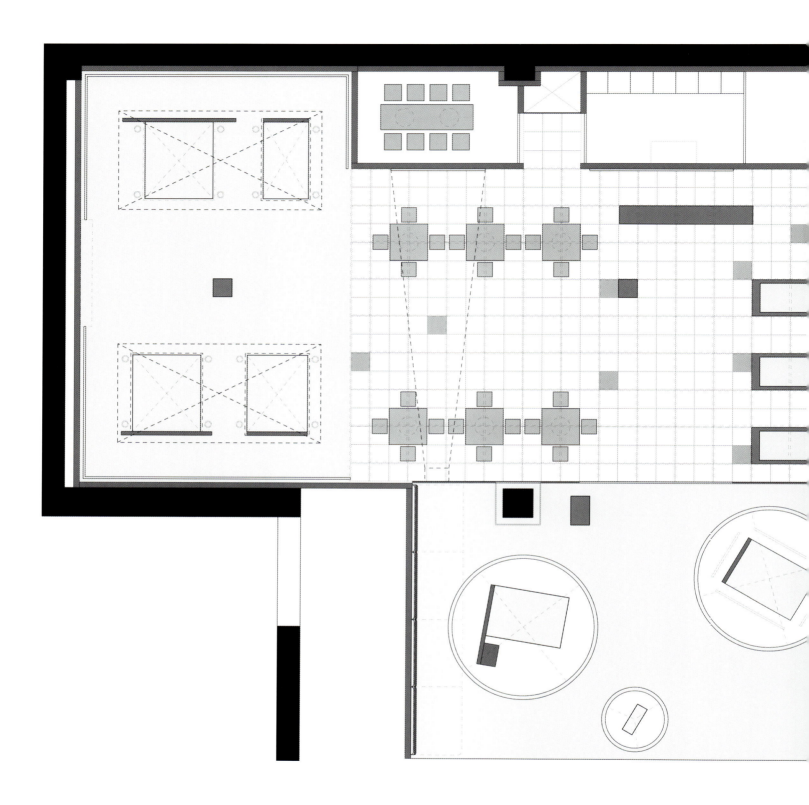

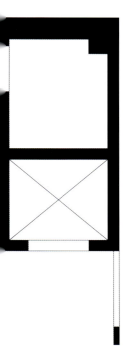

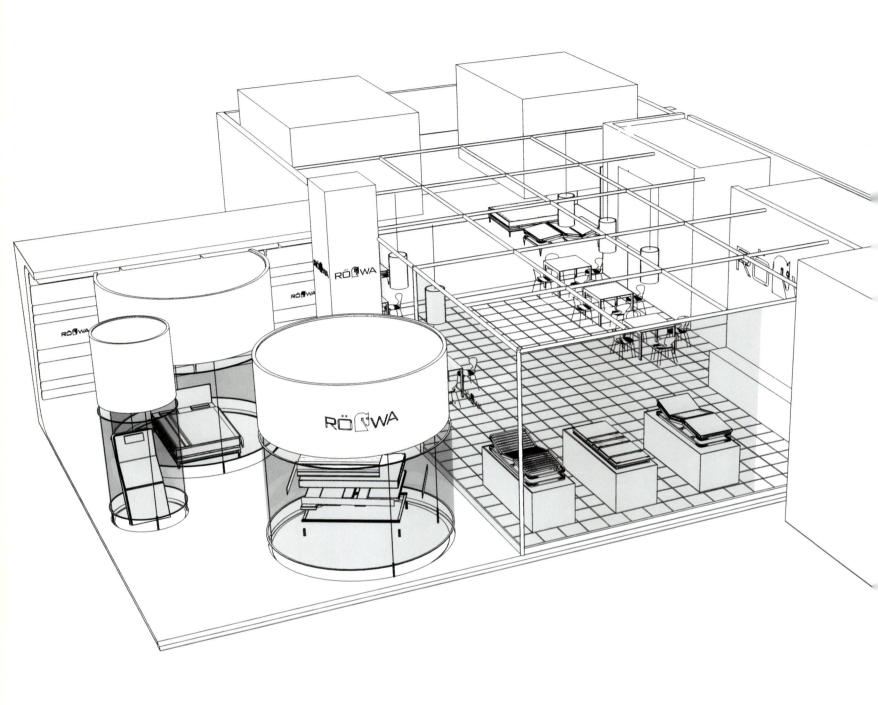

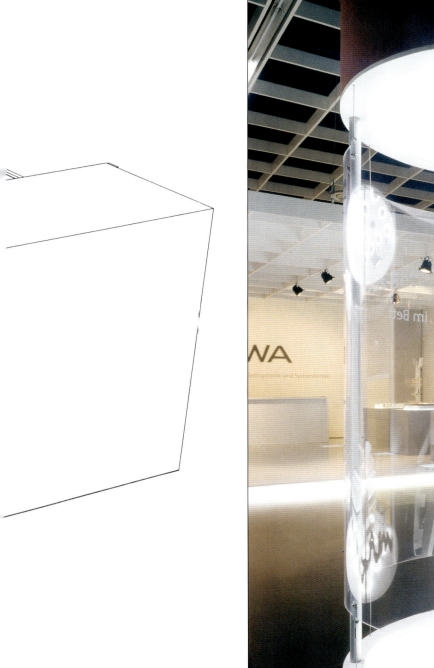

D'Art Design Gruppe

Philps Licht

EuroShop 2005, Düsseldorf, Germany

Royal Philips Electronics leads the market in lighting, diagnostic image systems, shaving machines, television sets, medical monitoring machines and silicone based systems. Philips Lighting is a division of Royal Philips Electronics, with general use lamps, halogen, fluorescent and high pressure arc lamps, indoor or outdoor, electronic, diode-based (LED), automobile lamps, or lamps for special requirements. Part of the challenge of this stand lies in the unification of the client's extremely varied products.

Targets: To state the worldwide leadership and innovative power of the enterprise by equaling the brand name and the phrase „consumer driven". To reinforce the "tribal experience", the design is focused on emotional participation.

Design concept: Lighthouse-Experience

"Mirror, mirror on the wall, who is brightest in all the land?" "Thou art the brightest in the street, but yonder lighthouse is infinitely prettier than you". "Why do my coffers remain empty when my goods are just as desirable?" asks the envious shop-owner. How to create the shopping atmosphere, in which the customer feels comfortable, has a good time and is glad to come back? Lighting is as meaningful for a perfect shopping experience as the display: this is the message from Philips Light. The passwords are "Enhance People's Lives with Lighting", or "Life is Light".

Describe the perfect shopping experience: A lighthouse in the endless sea of possible purchases, a stage to present the world of shopping in a new light.

"Experience the unique worlds we manufacture", says the brightly glowing "Big X" at the entrance of the Philips Lighthouse. Target groups aside, passion and fascination are open to all.

Fairy-tale readers plunge into the Master Color Gallery. Frog or King is the question that Mini Master illuminates at the first stage of the maze. "Grandma, why is it so bright here?" says the next space. "For me to see you better", says Master Color Elite, letting Little Red Riding Hood show her most brilliant colors. Around the corner the falcon and the wolf meet in the twilight, for only in twilight may lovers meet.

The realistic handyman is addressed too, with screwdrivers, saws and rubber boots standing parade. A sports car offers a realistic rush to a queue of enthusiastic drivers. Strollers eventually find the Chill out Patio Café, overlooking the lighthouse and the colorful patchwork of theatrical contrasts.

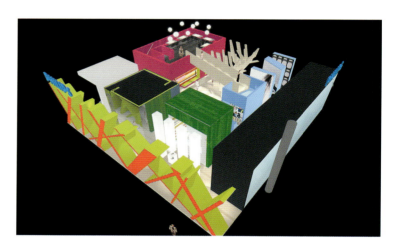

Photographs: contributed by por D'Art Design Gruppe

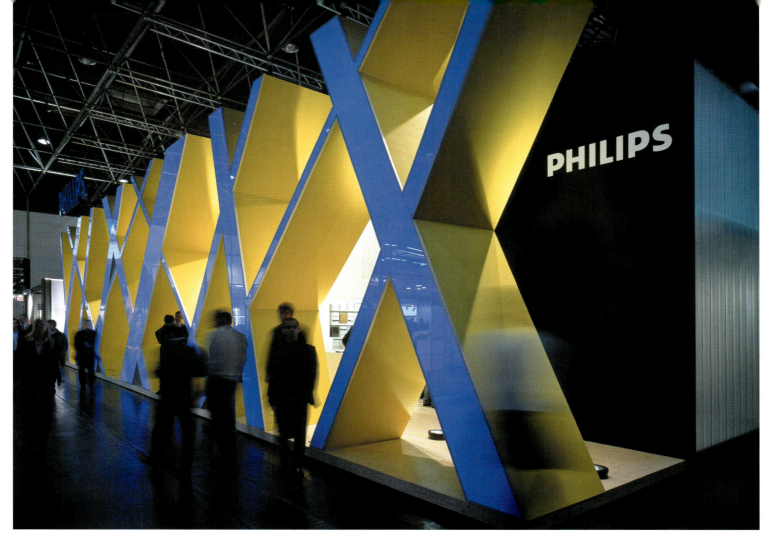

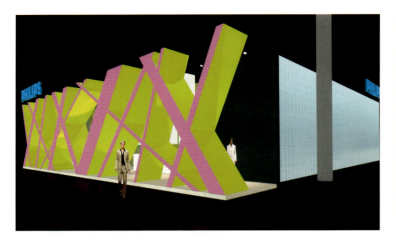

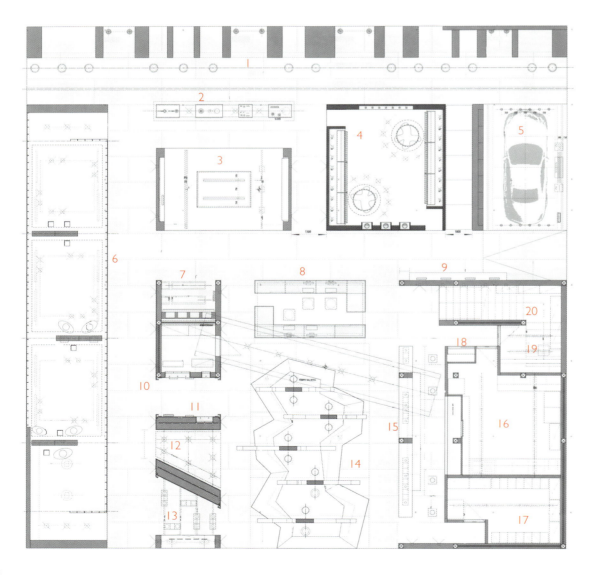

Ground floor plan

1. Big X
2. Product stations
3. Supermarket and DIY store
4. High end fashion store
5. Illuminated car
6. Master color room
7. Books store
8. Information desk
9. Light infocenter
10. Department store
11. Electronics store
12. Cosmetics store
13. Sports store
14. Patio area
15. Coffee bar
16. Catering
17. Storage
18. Wardrobe
19. Office
20. Technique

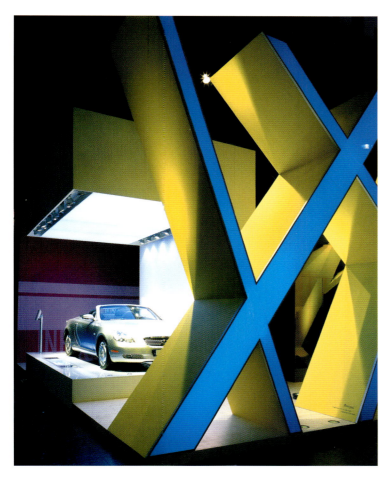

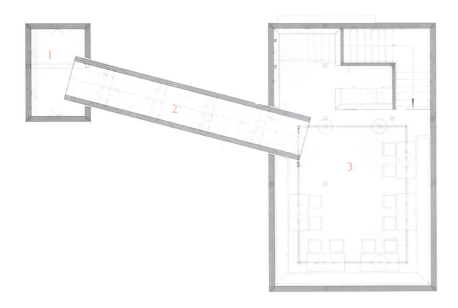

First floor plan

1. Viewpoint
2. Gangway
3. Communication area

127

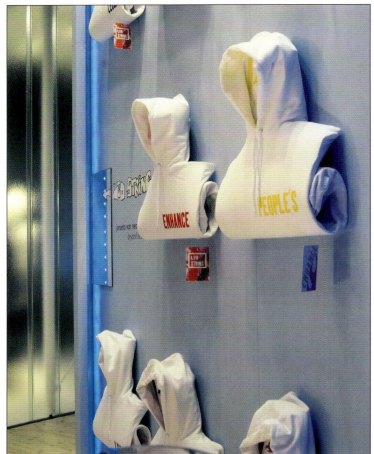

Vicente Sarrablo, Cristina Garcia & Jordi Roviras

DCPAL

Construmat 2005, Barcelona, Spain

The stand was to represent DCPAL, an enterprise dealing in unglazed ceramic materials (bricks, cobbles, pieces for aerated façades). The idea was to use their own products as the material to identify the space.

The main distinguishing feature was resolved with a ceramic curtain 4 m high, made out of a special type of cobble-like paving, which in one simple gesture zoned the space, separating or filtering the different area required (storage space, display area, an area of greater privacy).

On the floor, the same paving material is used to project the shadow of the curtain. Five lamps that pierce become display tables for the different colored bricks that are on show.

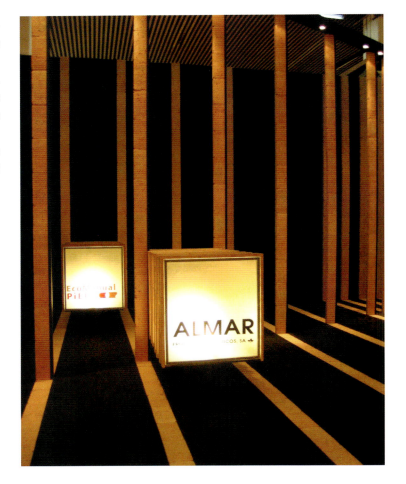

Photographs: Vicente Sarrablo

133

Main floor

1 Storage space
2 Counters and display surfaces for other materials
3 Masonry curtain made of ceramic cobbles
4 Stripes of ceramic cobbles as paving material
5 Lines of thin ceramic cobbles as paving material
6 Meeting table (private area)
7 Bar top (private area)
8 Vertical Tecnodad display case, by coperfil
9 Tradeshow key Construmat

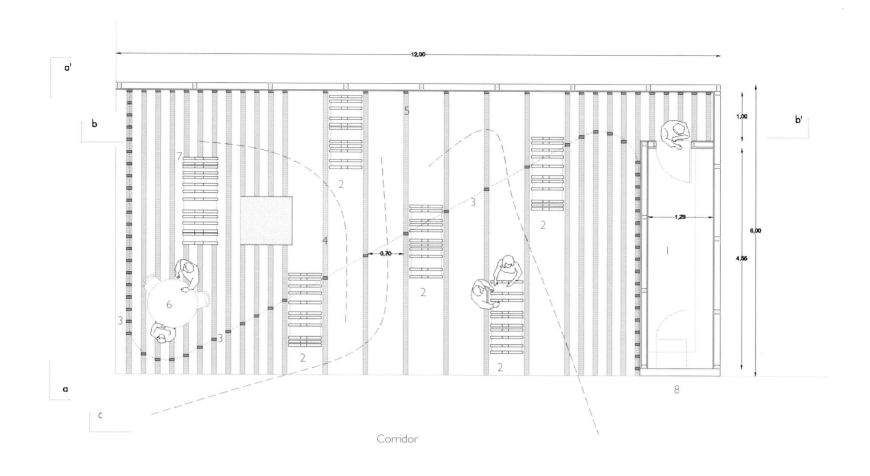

Corridor

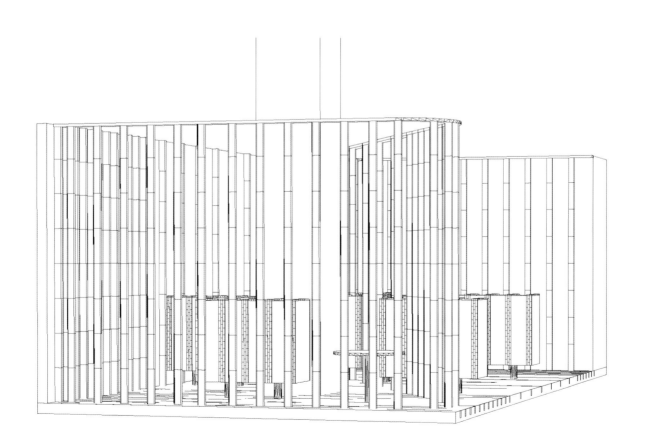

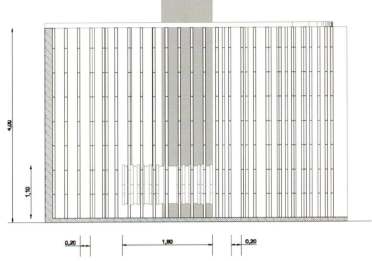

Section AA

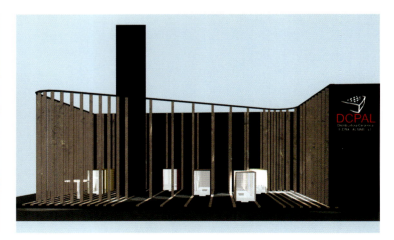

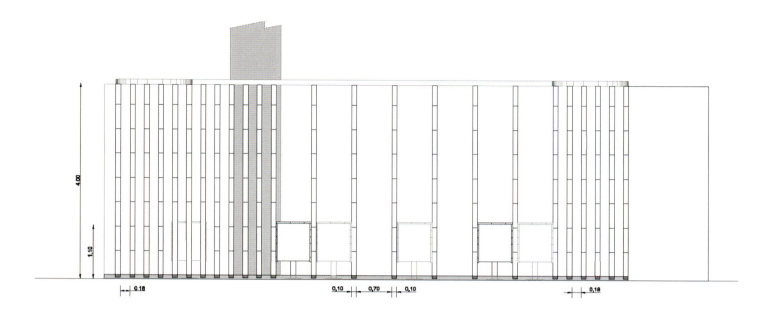

Section BB

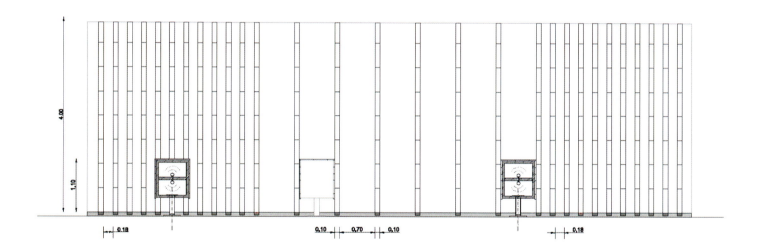

Section CC

Lorenc Yoo Design

Cushman & Wakefield

ICSC 2004, Las Vegas, USA

The client: Cushman & Wakefield - ICSC Las Vegas 2004 are a worldwide real estate services company with 11,000 employees, 51 offices in 51 countries and 6 continents.

The show: LYD is a design-only team in a context where the designs are given away to get the construction contract. The architectural and interior design approach brings another level of sensitivity to this arena...the mission to create jewels in a forest of predictability.

LYD does museums, exhibits for major corporations, with two to three trade show commissions a year...sometimes with immediate gratification, as this one was completed quicker than the graphic design for a brochure. Their project delivery time is usually between one year and five, so a definite change of pace occurred.

"More than one at a time of this kind of schedule would mean death or murder.... a very tense process so everyone needs a thick skin. We had our moments of emotion, but looking back it all turned out great... in the end. With the computer's ability to model virtual reality, clients forget the time and effort the making takes".

The project: LYD met with the client in NYC on April 9, on April 20 a design was presented for the installation of an exhibit in time for the ICSC show in Las Vegas May 15th. In the initial meeting it was understood the clients' intentions of promoting their international reach, facilitating social interaction: a sophisticated modern space, an outdoor café in a modern plaza, became the idea. The space had to allow 75 representatives to attend meetings. They wanted a barrier-free, welcoming space, which would project sophisticated expertise.

The cubical conference room was designed with a translucent roof and walls, raising it above the ground to give it lightness, a stretched fabric pavilion glowing ethereally from within, stable enough to carry three large-screen monitors outside. The plaza plan anchored all the components: the individual tables, bars and reception became soft-toned piano keys of carpet inlays. The red Vitra chairs and tables became a playful component. The ten property pylons became the perimetral boundary, making a visual gateway on 2 sides of the 35 foot by 50 foot space.

Furniture selection had to consider cost plus quick shipping. The design presented on April 20th survived almost intact, as the team went straight from the meeting to detailing, and furnished piecemeal sketches and details to lock in a price piece by piece. Design Within Reach Lighting and Vitra produced the pieces and the budget was met as well. Did the clients understand the achievement they demanded, or realize it was a major risk to expect delivery?

Photographs: Darris Harris - Padgett and Company Photograhy

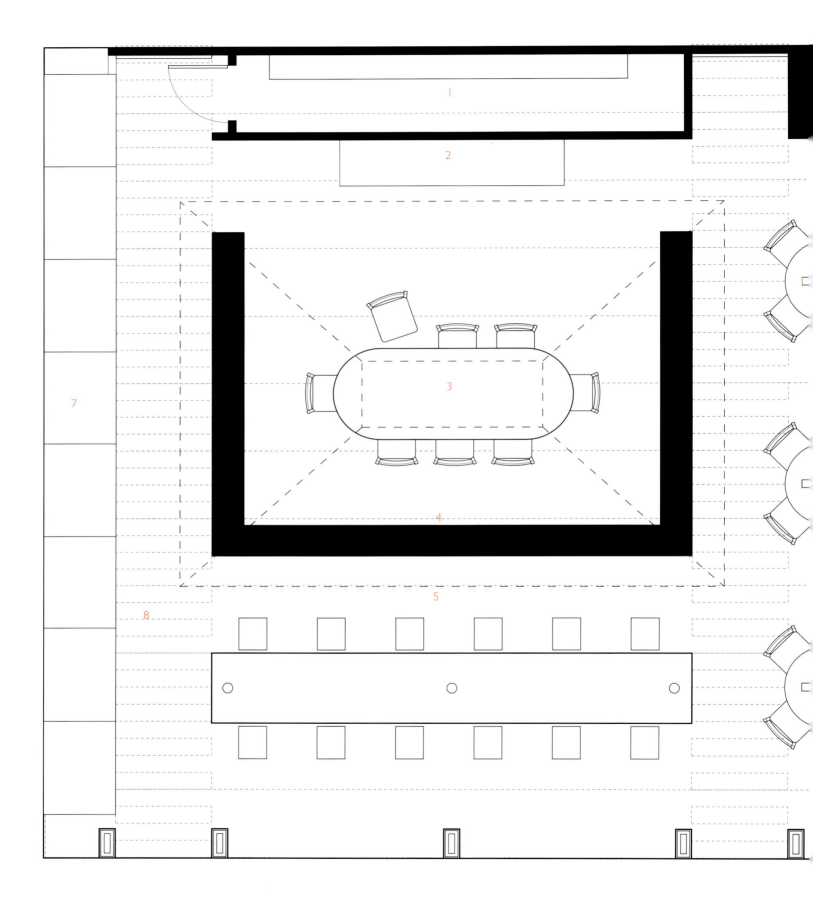

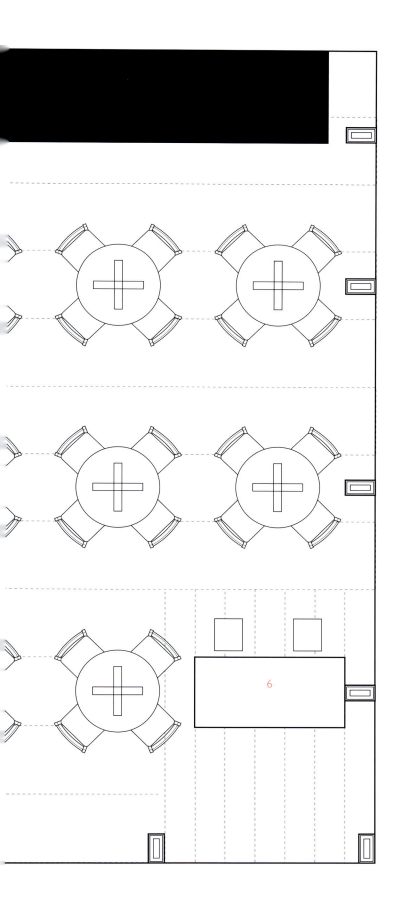

Plan

1. Storage
2. Buffet
3. Conference table
4. Tension fabric structure
5. Tension fabric ceiling / roof
6. Reception
7. Display wall
8. Carpet pattern

CUSHMAN &
WAKEFIELD

shopping mall

urban center

shopping mall

urban center

international presence

retail

outlet center

shopping mall

urban center

international presence

retail

outlet center

shopping mall

Brochure Cabinets

1. White vinyl text

2. Clear acrylic shelves supported by aluminum rod

3. Dark brown wood grain laminate similar to Laminart #3106-T
Wild ziricote textured

4. Laminart #9169-T Sky blue textured

5. Small wall to fill the gap between displays and back wall

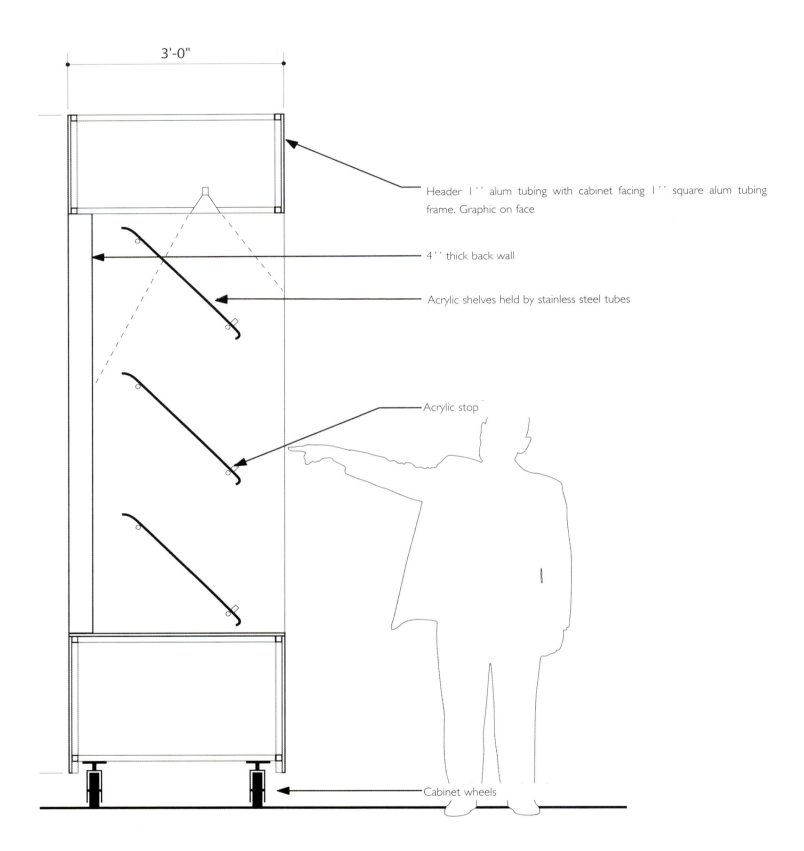

3'-0"

Header 1´´ alum tubing with cabinet facing 1´´ square alum tubing frame. Graphic on face

4´´ thick back wall

Acrylic shelves held by stainless steel tubes

Acrylic stop

Cabinet wheels

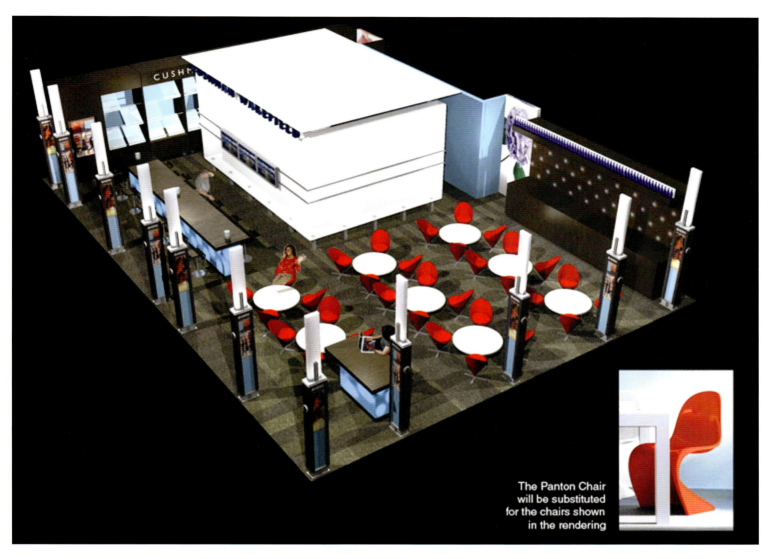

The Panton Chair will be substituted for the chairs shown in the rendering

Carpet plan

Reception table

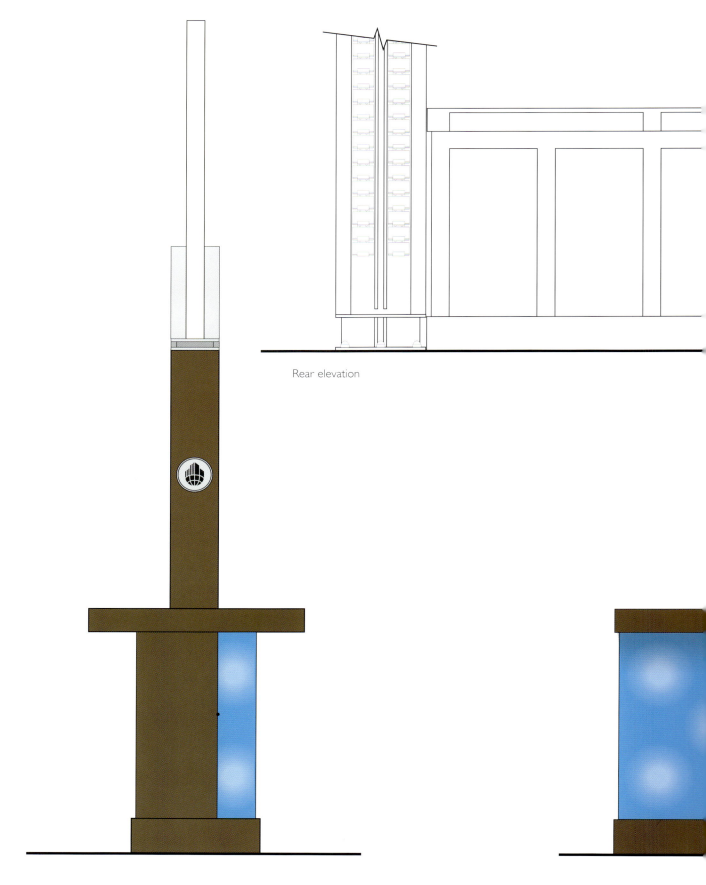

Rear elevation

Side elevation

Front elevation

146

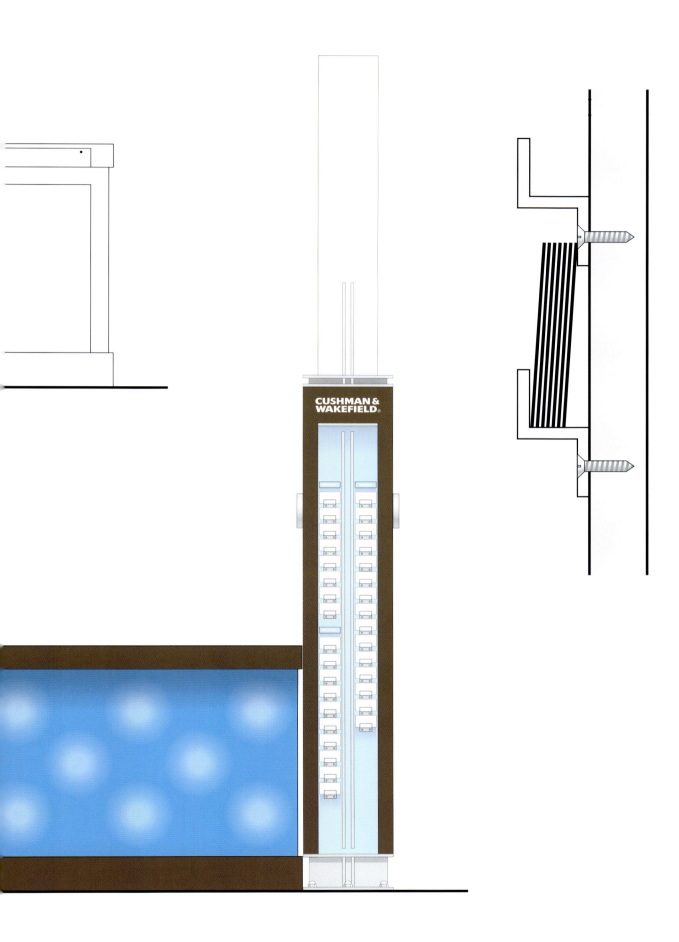

CUSHMAN & WAKEFIELD®

Formpol AG

Somfy

Swissbau 2005, Zurich, Switzerland

The new trend at tradeshows and events indicates a tendency to depart from the classical product displays, and seek a more emotional communication of what the customer has to gain. With their new stand, Somfy Switzerland follows suite. The stand's first public appearance was at the Zurich tradeshow Swissbau, in January 2005. Formpol, the design office, were requested to rethink the communication platform between Somfy Switzerland and their customers.

The international group Somfy is involved in the manufacture of motorized controls for shutters, venetian blinds or other sun shields. What distinguishes these products is the amount of know how they involve and the benefits they offer their owners, despite which they remain practically invisible for the user. Their quality is an exclusive function of their use and of the emotional well-being it produces. For example, when a building detects rain, it draws in the sun shields and parasols and closes the west-facing windows. Or at night, when the mere push of a button all the shutters close down and the whole building is safe from possible burglars; despite which, the following morning the first rays of the morning sun come in because the shutters have been raised at just the right moment.

At the Swissbau 2005, Comfy Switzerland used the catch phrase "Loft of Inspiration" to emphasize the experience offered by their automatic shutter control mechanism. In four loft type spaces the visitors discovered, as if it were a game, the possibilities of the Comfy controls panel. Each space adopted a different theme: the garden, the garage, the office or the home. The simulation of a whole day's passage in just 2 or 3 minutes, using light effects on the shutters, allowed the visitor to appreciate the benefits of the system. The visitor was able to intervene interactively in the process.

This will be the main concept of the Comfy Switzerland and Austria presentations at tradeshows during the next 2 or 3 years. Therefore, the stand was designed in modules so as to be easily adaptable to the changing situations. The system is based on a concealed network; thus, the partition system which contains the technical appliances can be assembled in a wide variety of ways. The images of atmospheric conditions attribute the necessary dramatic quality to the stand and lead the visitor to an emotional experience of the system's benefits. Additionally, the manufactured products are on display in the intermediate areas between the loft-type spaces, although they have a secondary role in the presentation. The spaces for information and communication contain a reception desk and a bar area.

Photographs: Brigitte Richi

Telis 4 RTS

Telis 4 RTS

Telis 4 RTS

Telis 4 RTS

D'Art Design Gruppe

D'Art Design Gruppe

EuroShop 2005, Düsseldorf, Germany

At EuroShop 2005, the world's largest trade fair dedicated to the investment needs of the retail sector, more than 1,500 exhibitors present themselves from February 19 to 23, 2005, in more than 200,000 m² of halls. In this context, the biggest international tour de force for trade fair stand construction/design and event management takes place in the EuroExpo area.

The task at hand is the presentation of D'Art Design Gruppe at EuroShop 2005 in Düsseldorf. The company is to showcase itself with an emphasis on its core competencies in all areas of corporate and brand communications, especially in concept development and realization of trade fair, shop and communications design projects.

The goal is to support the positioning of D'Art Design Gruppe as a leading design agency for innovative communications with pan-European operations. The unique challenge is to convey a tangible experience of the company as a service provider for creative ideas - and above all, to inspire visitors to become directly involved in an interactive experience of D'Art Design Gruppe.

"The whole is greater than the sum of its parts," or as Goethe put it in Faust, "How all things live and work, and ever blending, weave one vast whole from being's ample range!" Patchwork or sample - that's the key message D'Art Design Gruppe has chosen for its appearance this year at the trade fair EuroShop 2005. Consciously and deliberately, the stand presents the visitor with a piece of wisdom that everyone has known all along. Because there can be nothing greater than cooperation and interaction between individuals: that's D'Art Design Gruppe.

As its name suggests, a patchwork is made up of many elements, and so is the trade fair presentation of D'Art Design Gruppe. So-called Samples - stations in the form of specially designed counters - show details and excerpts from the fascinating world of D'Art Design Gruppe. A colorful potpourri, that breaks the creative agency down into many small facets, revealing its true character. Just as light isn't simply white either, but composed of an infinite number of color shades.

To find D'Art, the visitor must embark on a voyage of discovery through a labyrinth of Samples. Basic human instincts are a trusty guide. Hunt and gather, sample and hold. And who can help but love it? Useful, useless, shameless and senseless objects: at trade fairs, we hunt and gather anything and everything we can get a hold of. In our case, the visitor is invited to collect and take home the company itself! For each Sample, there is a corresponding brochure, which gives background information on the exhibits. Curious visitors can get to know D'Art Design GruppeE and its philosophy best at the oversized table soccer game: living proof that the grass is greener where the good ideas grow. More insight into art for (D')ART's sake can be found at the longest news ticker ever. Doesn't a rose smell just as sweet? Sure, and still waters run wet.

Examples of projects and references are of course a must. How about a Barbie kitchen, Herr WMF? A Gauloises, Mademoiselle Renault? A pair of handcuffs for your handbag, Ms. Samsonite? Sounds and sensations envelope the eager collector at the Press Sample, where a sonorous voice breathes life into clever D'ART literary musings. Buzz, little bee, fly around ... "Beetronic" means a bee in your bonnet when it comes to visions: concealed artistic passions, awakened as architecture of the future. - If you need a break from the thrill of the hunt, you can relax with a cool drink in the shade of a box tree hedge. But there's an American drag race car waiting for every adrenaline junky up for a duel. Gentlemen, start your engines!

At the end of the course, having reached the final destination of a journey with 16 stations, the visitor is in possession of the entire company. And now it's your turn: sample and hold.

Photographs: contributed by D'Art Design Gruppe

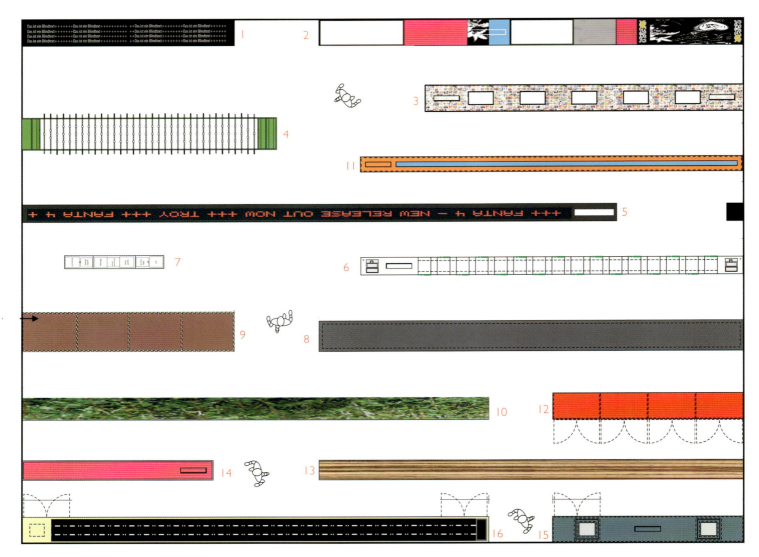

1. Lighting table, Signalization
2 Project documentation, Philips
3. Promotions + x-mas
4. Football player / Philosophy
5. Crew / LED – running letters
6. Shelves / Archive
7. Press
8. Bench

9. Packing table
10 Hedge / Laurel tree
11 Transparent tape "Beetronic"
12 Logistics
13 Counter
14 Awards
15 Website
16 Roadway

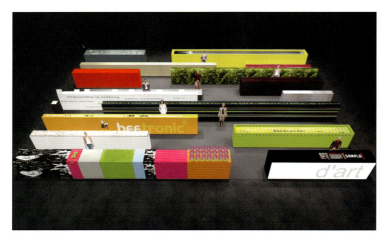

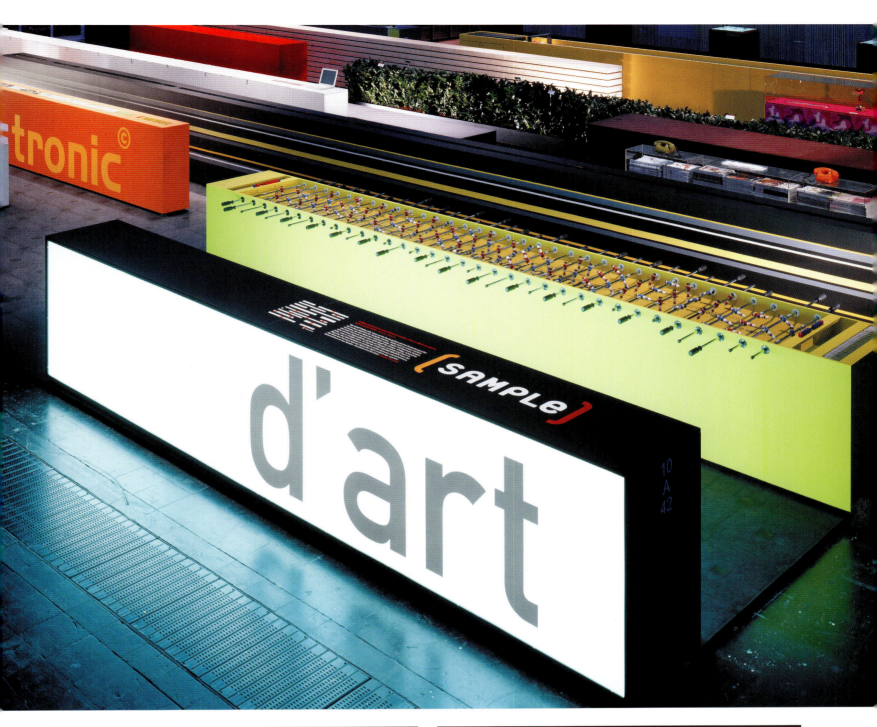

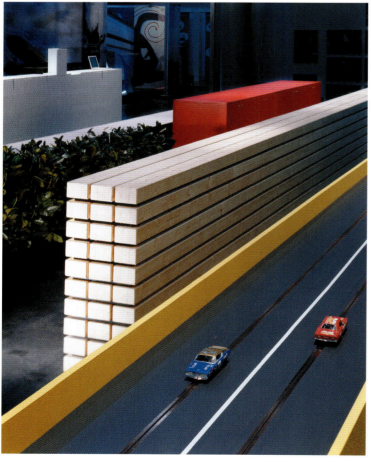

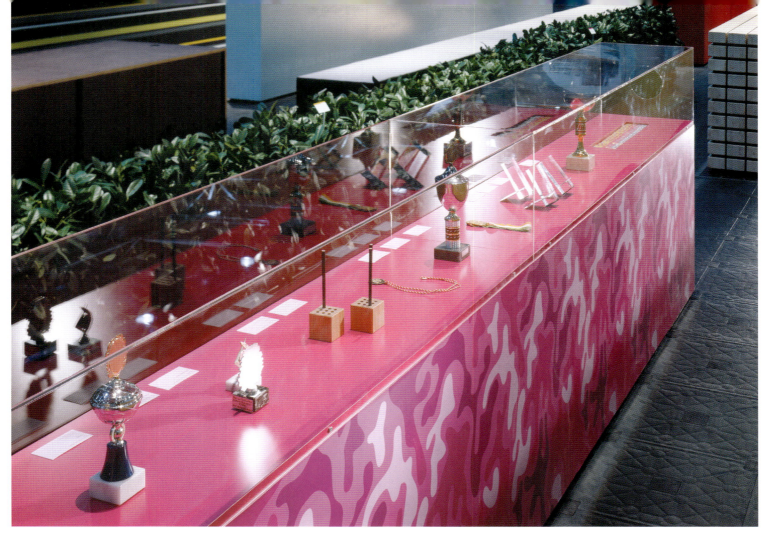

Kurz und Partner Architekten

HS Schoch GmbH

International Automobil Exhibition 2004, Hannover, Germany

The trade fair appearance of HS Schoch, Metec and EBLA were brought into a common spatial context. Kurz und Partner Architekten developed a way to present the three as independent and qualified partners in one combination. In the architectural language the parallelism of the three production lines is translated into linear elements. The liness are the main design element and symbolize the three companies with their three colors. The linear elements act as an enormous eye catcher. The whole stand architecture is continuously and consequently built upon this design element.

The lines develop into:
- Product presentation
- Seating opportunities
- Counter elements
- Carry media equipment
- Graphic style

The interplay and the combination of the companies and their products show the whole bandwidth of a systems supplier.

The continuation of the lines on the rear wall also guarantees the long-range effect and attracts the attention of the visitors. The lines interrupt the visitor stream along the main aisle and pull the visitors into the exhibition area.

Photographs: Thomas Küppers

ICE-Trennwand

Schottwandeinbau für DB Reisezug ICE 2
Glasfaserverstärkter Kunststoff (GFK) im
Handlaminatverfahren hergestellt
Designmodifikation an Zuginterieur
Wandstärken bis 8 mm!
Brandschutz nach DIN 5510 S4/SR2/ST2

ICE Partition Wall

Partition wall installation for German Rail
Passenger Train ICE 2
Glass-fiber reinforced plastics, made in manual
laminating process
Design modification for interior of train
Wall thickness up to 8 mm!
Fire protection acc. to DIN 5510 S4/SR2/ST2

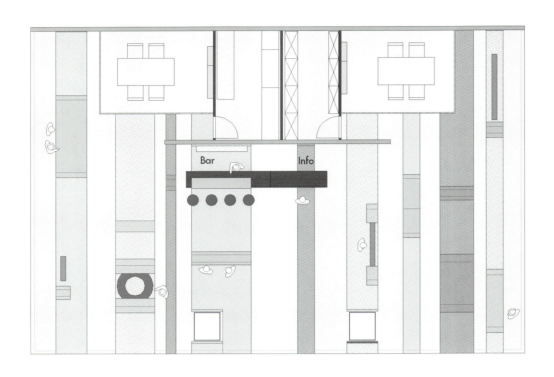

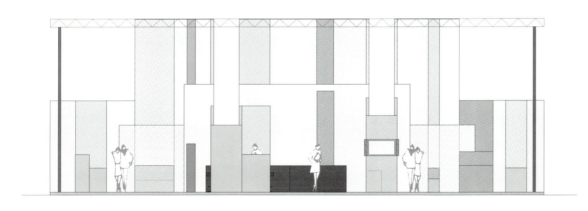

Arno Design

Sto AG

Farbe 2005, Cologne, Germany

Sto AG, worldwide leaders in the field of insulation, considered their presence at FARBE essential to introduce their latest innovations, celebrate their 50th year in business and present the Sto-Foundation. Arno Design GmbH, Münich, have been handling Sto AG's trade show stands for some 15 years, and know their client thoroughly.

The Sto Communication and Information Lounge took up 596 sq.m of floor space in hall 11-2. The distribution of the exhibition space was inspired on the layout of a minigolf course. A symbolic structure in the form of two six-meter-high translucent towers acted as a landmark; its Sto-yellow glowing facets aroused the visitors attention and drew them to the space. Around them, grouped as if by chance, were 15 communication islands with dynamically arranged seating accommodation in different color groups. Each color area presented a particular Sto-theme: Orange for StoTherm Classic, Blue for Photocatalytical Colors, Red for Diabolo, a Painter's Software and Yellow for the Sto Foundation. The 45 cm-high benches invited visitors to feel comfortable at the Sto stand.

Arno Design blurred the functional character of the luminous signs throughout the Sto-itinerary and made them grow straight out of the seating. Swiveling light boxes and well-placed luminous forms strategically underlined the communication hall's overall illumination, gently reflected by the pale gray floor. A dazzlingly white banner hung from the ceiling, describing a dynamic line flowing through the stand; slogans or words printed or projected on it brought the visitor smoothly towards the Sto Information Lounge where a product presentation started every 30 minutes. TV moderator Ronny Meyer was employed by Sto AG to acquaint the public with the highlights of the stand and lead them through it in a comfortably informative manner.

In-depth information was provided by Plasma screens installed in each thematic area. At the exit of the information and communication areas, Sto personnel were available to have a relaxed explanatory talk about what had been seen and heard, either at the circular bar, the interview booths, or the numerous coffee tables.

The stands features such as the yellow towers, the red, yellow, or blue seating and the display walls were designed especially for the show. Some elements, like the Sto-yellow light boxes will be used in future Sto-events.

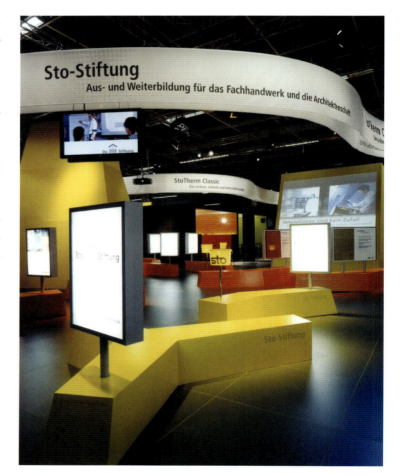

Photographs: Frank Kotzerke

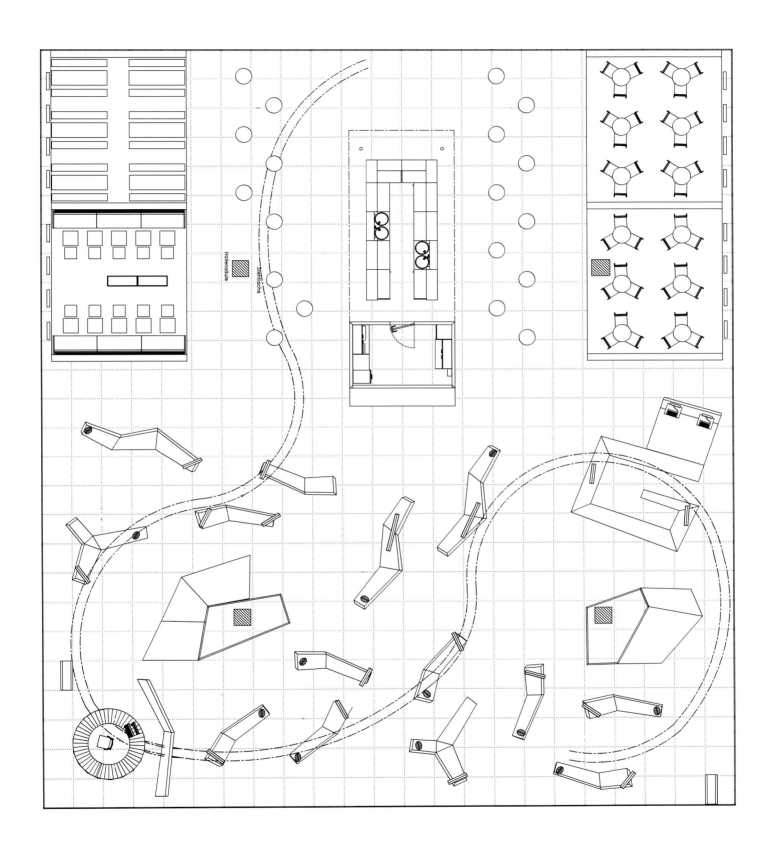

Hallensäule

Stehtische

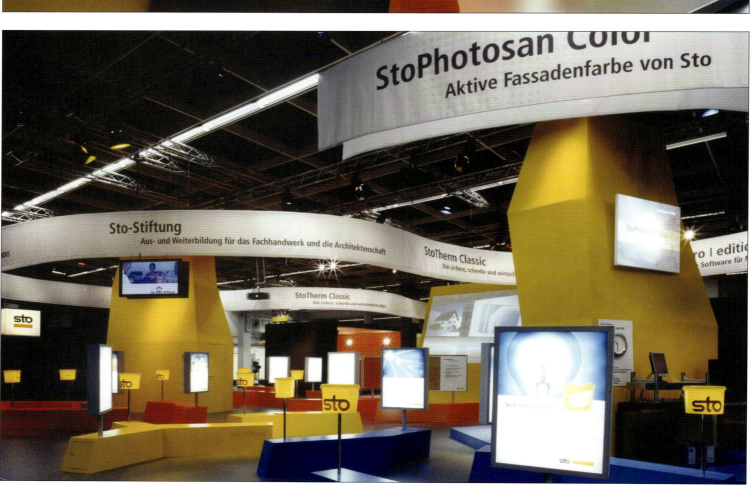

Schimdhuber + Partner

KMS

Mediacloud

CeBIT 2005, Hanover, Germany

Since 2002 the stands of the cellphone company O2 Germany have been a joyful presence at tradeshows. This year's spectacular installation by the Munich office KMS Team and Schmidhuber+Partner, stressed the CeBIT 2005. The thing is called "Mediacloud", a world premiere attracting all the attention: a 1,000 sq.m projection screen hovering about 3 or 4 m. above the spectators' heads.

The motion pictures on it are produced by 28.000 light points; the 20 cm space between them is set so the eye can fill the gaps and perceive a complete image. It is built out of plastic tubes 4.5 cm in diameter that hang down from the hall's ceiling and are closed off with a matt plastic diffuser. The light of the RGB-light-diodes is monitored from a central computer. The technology involved was developed especially for the "Mediacloud Project" in Germany, USA and Taiwan. The phenomenon is not only the largest color image screen in the world, but also a visually interesting sculpture. The different lengths of the tubes generate an undulated surface, so the visitor has the impression of being underneath a blue cloud, over which moving pictures glide.

Under the Mediacloud are the typical O2 lounges which unfold into three separate raised desks. The newest O2 products are presented in specific areas dedicated to "Entertainment", "Communication" or "Business". The swaying and glowing pedestals can be sat on or, on an upper floor, there may be deckchairs (Entertainment), a Bar (Communication) or the white cubic stools and low tables, for cellphones or Laptops (Business). The desks are finished in white synthetic flooring that contrasts with the shaggy petroleum colored carpets.

A central axis connects various service points: from Reception to Shop to Customer Service, past a "Juice Bar" where cellphones can be recharged, through the two cafeterias upstairs, to end as the writing table in the executive office.

Trade visitors have a generously dimensioned lounge by the main access to the desks on the ground floor. The cafeteria is above. The generous deployment of glass walls and balustrades, underlined by lighting, establish flowing connections between areas and levels, allowing the constructions to intersect easily.

Photographs: Wolfgang Oberle, München

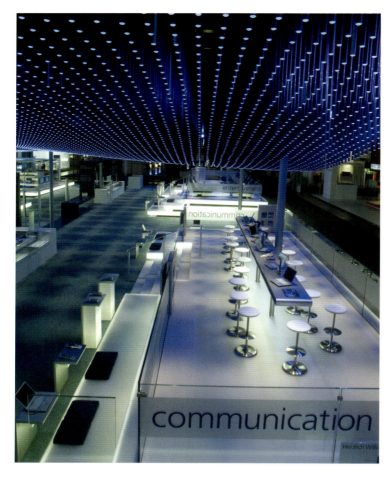